MW01137924

VIRGIL: SELECTIONS FROM AENEID VI

CAMBRIDGE LATIN TEXTS

VIRGIL

SELECTIONS FROM
AENEID VI

with a further selection from the English
translation of C. Day Lewis

ANNE HAWARD
New Hall School, Chelmsford

CAMBRIDGE
UNIVERSITY PRESS

PUBLISHED BY THE PRESS SYNDICATE OF THE UNIVERSITY OF CAMBRIDG
The Pitt Building, Trumpington Street, Cambridge, United Kingdom

CAMBRIDGE UNIVERSITY PRESS
The Edinburgh Building, Cambridge CB2 2RU, UK
40 West 20th Street, New York, NY 10011–4211, USA
477 Williamstown Road, Port Melbourne, VIC 3207, Australia
Ruiz de Alarcón 13, 28014 Madrid, Spain
Dock House, The Waterfront, Cape Town 8001, South Africa

http://www.cambridge.org

First published 1983
Fourth printing 1996
Ninth printing 2003

Printed in the United Kingdom at the University Press, Cambridge

Library of Congress catalogue card number 82–12760

British Library Cataloguing in Publication Data
Virgil
[Aeneid. Book 6. *English & Latin. Selections*].
Virgil : selections from Aeneid VI. – (Cambridge
Latin texts)
1. Latin poetry
I. Title II. Haward, Anne
873'.01   PA6125

ISBN 0 521 28694 8

ACKNOWLEDGEMENTS

The Latin text is taken from the Oxford Classical Texts edition of *Vergili Opera* edited by R.A.B. Mynors, © Oxford University Press 1969. Reprinted by permission of Oxford University Press.

The English text is taken from *The Aeneid of Virgil*, translated by C. Day Lewis, and is reproduced by permission of The Executors of the Estate of C. Day Lewis and Chatto & Windus Ltd. Reprinted by permission of A.D. Peters & Co. Ltd.

Map drawn by Reg Piggott.

The cover illustration is from a red figure vase depicting Hercules and Cerberus and is reproduced by courtesy of the Mansell Collection.

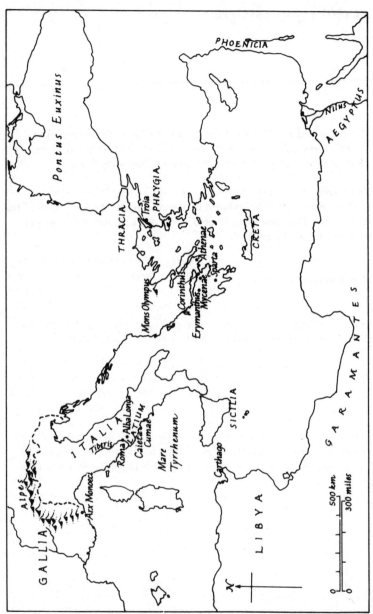

The Mediterranean, showing places mentioned in *Aeneid* VI

On the night that Troy was finally captured by the Greeks, Aeneas was told in a vision that he must found a new city. Taking his aged father, Anchises, and his little son, Iulus, Aeneas and a band of Trojans escaped from Troy. Creusa, Aeneas' wife, was lost but the rest of the party reached the mountains, where they built ships to sail to the West.

Aeneas tried to found his new city in Thrace and again in Crete; each time signs from the gods drove him westwards until after many adventures he reached Sicily. After the death there of Anchises, the Trojans set sail again but a storm shipwrecked them at Carthage in North Africa. Here the beautiful queen Dido had recently settled; she welcomed Aeneas and hoped to keep him there as her husband. Aeneas stayed all winter with Dido until he was warned by Jupiter that he was ignoring his divinely appointed task. Dido passionately begged him to stay, but Aeneas and his men sailed for Sicily; heartbroken, Dido killed herself. From Sicily the Trojans crossed to Italy, the Western Land foretold to Aeneas, and landed near Cumae.

At the beginning of Book VI Aeneas goes to the Sibyl, priestess of Apollo, to discover his future fate. He asks to descend to the Underworld to see his father, Anchises, and learn what destiny Italy holds for him. The Sibyl orders him to rid himself and his fleet of pollution by holding the funeral of a dead comrade and then to search out the Golden Bough which will gain him admission to Hades. Aeneas carries out these commands with the help of his mother, the goddess Venus, and enters the cave which leads down to the Underworld.

This done, Aeneas hastened to follow the Sibyl's directions.
A deep, deep cave there was, its mouth enormously gaping,
Shingly, protected by the dark lake and the forest gloom:
Above it, no winged creatures could ever wing their way
With impunity, so lethal was the miasma which
Went fuming up from its black throat to the vault of heaven:
Wherefore the Greeks called it Avernus, the Birdless Place.
Here the Sibyl first lined up four black-skinned bullocks,
Poured a libation of wine upon their foreheads, and then,
Plucking the topmost hairs from between their brows, she placed
These on the altar fires as an initial offering,
Calling aloud upon Hecate, powerful in heaven and hell.
While others laid their knives to these victims' throats, and caught
The fresh warm blood in bowls, Aeneas sacrificed
A black-fleeced lamb to Night, the mother of the Furies,
And her great sister, Earth, and a barren heifer to Proserpine.
Then he set up altars by night to the god of the Underworld,
Laying upon the flames whole carcases of bulls
And pouring out rich oil over the burning entrails.
But listen! — at the very first crack of dawn, the ground
Underfoot began to mutter, the woody ridges to quake,
And a baying of hounds was heard through the half-light: the
    goddess was coming,
Hecate. The Sibyl cried: —
                    Away! Now stand away,
You uninitiated ones, and clear the whole grove!
But you, Aeneas, draw your sword from the scabbard and fare forth!
Now you need all your courage, your steadfastness of heart.
    So much she said and, ecstatic, plunged into the opened cave mouth:
Unshrinking went Aeneas step for step with his guide.
    You gods who rule the kingdom of souls! You soundless shades!
Chaos, and Phlegethon! O mute wide leagues of Nightland! —
Grant me to tell what I have heard! With your assent
May I reveal what lies deep in the gloom of the Underworld!

Ibant obscuri sola sub nocte per umbram
perque domos Ditis vacuas et inania regna: 270
quale per incertam lunam sub luce maligna
est iter in silvis, ubi caelum condidit umbra
Iuppiter, et rebus nox abstulit atra colorem.
vestibulum ante ipsum primisque in faucibus Orci
Luctus et ultrices posuere cubilia Curae,
pallentesque habitant Morbi tristisque Senectus, 275
et Metus et malesuada Fames ac turpis Egestas,
terribiles visu formae, Letumque Labosque;
tum consanguineus Leti Sopor et mala mentis
Gaudia, mortiferumque adverso in limine Bellum,
ferreique Eumenidum thalami et Discordia demens 280
vipereum crinem vittis innexa cruentis.
in medio ramos annosaque bracchia pandit
ulmus opaca, ingens, quam sedem Somnia vulgo
vana tenere ferunt, foliisque sub omnibus haerent.
multaque praeterea variarum monstra ferarum, 285
Centauri in foribus stabulant Scyllaeque biformes
et centumgeminus Briareus ac belua Lernae
horrendum stridens, flammisque armata Chimaera,
Gorgones Harpyiaeque et forma tricorporis umbrae.
corripit hic subita trepidus formidine ferrum 290
Aeneas strictamque aciem venientibus offert,

2

obscūrus dark, dim, *here* = in the darkness
Dis, m. the god Dis or Pluto, lord of the Underworld
270 quālis such as, like
quāle ... est iter such as a journey is
malignus grudging
condere hide
abstulit: auferre take away
āter black
color, m. colour
faucēs, f.pl. jaws, entrance
Orcus, m. the Underworld
Lūctus, m. Grief
ultrīx avenging
posuēre = posuērunt
cubīle, n. bed, lair
275 pallēns pale
Senectūs, f. Old Age
malesuādus evil-counselling
Famēs, f. Hunger
turpis disgraceful, foul
Egestās, f. Need, Poverty
terribilēs visū fōrmae shapes dreadful to behold
Lētum, n. Death
Labōs, m. Toil
cōnsanguineus of the same blood, brother
Sopor, m. Sleep
mortifer death-bringing
adversus facing, opposite
280 ferreus made of iron
Eumenides, f.pl. the Furies
thalamus, m. chamber
Discordia, f. Discord, Strife
dēmēns mad
vīpereus snaky
crīnem ... innexa having bound her hair
vitta, f. headband
cruentus bloody
rāmus, m. bough
annōsus aged
pandere spread

ulmus, f. elm
opācus shady, dark
sēdēs, f. resting-place, home
vulgō ... ferunt they commonly say
285 *quam sedem vulgo ferunt Somnia vana tenere*
folium, n. leaf
haerēre stick, cling
praetereā besides
fera, f. wild beast
Centaurus, m. the Centaur, half man and half horse
forēs, f.pl. door
stabulāre be stabled
Scylla, f. Scylla, half woman and half sea-monster
bifōrmis of two shapes
centumgeminus hundredfold
Briareus, m. Briareus, a giant with a hundred arms
bēlua Lernae the beast of Lerna (near Argos), the Hydra (a many-headed water-serpent)
horrendum dreadfully
strīdere hiss
armāre arm
Chimaera, f. the Chimaera, a fire-breathing monster, part lion, part goat, part snake
Gorgones, f.pl. the Gorgons, three hideous sisters, whose gaze turned men to stone
Harpȳiae, f.pl. the Harpies, half women and half vultures
fōrma tricorporis umbrae the shape of a three-bodied shade, the monster Geryon
290 corripere seize
trepidus alarmed
formīdō, f. fear
ferrum, n. sword
strictam: stringere draw, unsheathe
aciēs, f. edge, blade, battle line
strictam aciem (monstris) venientibus offert

3

et ni docta comes tenues sine corpore vitas
admoneat volitare cava sub imagine formae,
inruat et frustra ferro diverberet umbras.
Hinc via Tartarei quae fert Acherontis ad undas.   295
turbidus hic caeno vastaque voragine gurges
aestuat atque omnem Cocyto eructat harenam.
portitor has horrendus aquas et flumina servat
terribili squalore Charon, cui plurima mento
canities inculta iacet, stant lumina flamma,   300
sordidus ex umeris nodo dependet amictus.
ipse ratem conto subigit velisque ministrat
et ferruginea subvectat corpora cumba,
iam senior, sed cruda deo viridisque senectus.
huc omnis turba ad ripas effusa ruebat,   305
matres atque viri defunctaque corpora vita
magnanimum heroum, pueri innuptaeque puellae,
impositique rogis iuvenes ante ora parentum:
quam multa in silvis autumni frigore primo
lapsa cadunt folia, aut ad terram gurgite ab alto   310
quam multae glomerantur aves, ubi frigidus annus
trans pontum fugat et terris immittit apricis.
stabant orantes primi transmittere cursum
tendebantque manus ripae ulterioris amore.
navita sed tristis nunc hos nunc accipit illos,   315
ast alios longe summotos arcet harena.
Aeneas miratus enim motusque tumultu
'dic,' ait, 'o virgo, quid vult concursus ad amnem?
quidve petunt animae? vel quo discrimine ripas
hae linquunt, illae remis vada livida verrunt ?'   320

ni = nisi
doctus learned
comes, m.f. companion
tenuis thin, insubstantial
admonēre warn
volitāre fly, flutter
cavus hollow
imāgō, f. form, likeness
inruere rush at
ni docta comes ... admoneat ...,
   (Aeneas) inruat
dīverberāre slash, carve up
295 *hinc (est) via*
Tartareus of Tartarus, the Underworld
ferre *here* = lead
Acherōn, m. the Acheron, one of the
   seven rivers of the Underworld
turbidus confused, thick
caenum, n. mud
vāstus huge
vorāgō, f. abyss, chasm
gurges, m. whirlpool, flood
aestuāre boil, seethe
Cōcȳtus, m. the river Cocytus in the
   Underworld
ēructāre throw up
harēna, f. sand
portitor, m. ferryman
servāre look after, guard
squālor, m. filth, dirt
Charōn, m. Charon
mentum, n. chin
300 cānitiēs, f. grey hair
incultus untrimmed, unkempt
stāre *here* = be fixed, stare
lūmen, n. light, *here* pl. = eyes
nōdus, m. knot
dēpendēre hang down
amictus, m. cloak
ratis, f. boat
contus, m. pole
subigere push along
vēlum, n. sail
ministrāre attend to
ferrūgineus rust-coloured, dark

subvectāre carry
cumba, f. boat
crūdus fresh, vigorous
viridis green
305 effūsa: effundere pour out
dēfūncta: dēfungī + Form E
   (ablative) finish with, end
magnanimus great-spirited
hērōs, m. hero
innūptus unwed
rogus, m. funeral pyre
autumnus, m. autumn
frīgus, n. cold
quam multa ... folia cadunt
311 glomerāre gather together, flock
avis, f. bird
aut quam multae aves ad terram ab
   gurgite alto glomerantur
frīgidus icy, cold
pontus, m. sea
fugāre put to flight, drive
immittere send into
aprīcus sunny
trānsmittere cursum to make the
   crossing
tendere stretch out
ulterior further
315 nāvita = nauta
ast = at
summovēre move away, send away
arcēre + Form E (ablative) keep
   away from
aliōs longē summōtōs arcet others he
   moves far away and keeps from,
   lit. others, moved far away, he
   keeps from
ait he said
vult *here* = means, signifies
concursus, m. gathering
amnis, m. river
-ve or
discrimen, n. distinction
320 vada, n.pl. shallows
līvidus lead-coloured, dark
verrere sweep

5

olli sic breviter fata est longaeva sacerdos:
'Anchisa generate, deum certissima proles,
Cocyti stagna alta vides Stygiamque paludem,
di cuius iurare timent et fallere numen.
haec omnis, quam cernis, inops inhumataque turba est;   325
portitor ille Charon; hi, quos vehit unda, sepulti.
nec ripas datur horrendas et rauca fluenta
transportare prius quam sedibus ossa quierunt.
centum errant annos volitantque haec litora circum;
tum demum admissi stagna exoptata revisunt.'   330
constitit Anchisa satus et vestigia pressit
multa putans sortemque animo miseratus iniquam.

He saw there, sorrowing because deprived of death's fulfilment,   333
Leucaspis and Orontes, the commodore of the Lycian
Squadron, who had gone down, their ship being lost with all hands
In a squall, sailing with him the stormy seas from Troy.
    And look! yonder was roaming the helmsman, Palinurus,
Who, on their recent voyage, while watching the stars, had fallen
From the afterdeck, thrown off the ship there in mid-passage.
A sombre form in the deep shadows, Aeneas barely
Recognised him; then accosted: —
                              Which of the gods, Palinurus,
Snatched you away from us and made you drown in the mid-sea?
Oh, tell me! For Apollo, whom never before had I found
Untruthful, did delude my mind with this one answer, ⁻
Foretelling that you would make your passage to Italy
Unharmed by sea. Is it thus he fulfils a sacred promise?
    Palinurus replied: —
                         The oracle of Phoebus has not tricked you,
My captain, son of Anchises; nor was I drowned by a god.
It was an accident: I slipped, and the violent shock
Of my fall broke off the tiller to which I was holding firmly
As helmsman, and steering the ship. By the wild seas I swear
That not on my own account was I frightened nearly so much as
Lest your ship, thus crippled, its helmsman overboard,
Lose steerage-way and founder amid the mountainous waves.
Three stormy nights did the South wind furiously drive me along
Over the limitless waters: on the fourth day I just

6

olli = illi
fārī speak
longaevus aged
Anchīsā generāte sprung from/son
    of Anchises
deum = deōrum
prōlēs, f. offspring
stāgnum, n. pool
Stygius Stygian, of the Styx (a river
    in the Underworld)
palūs, f. marsh
iūrāre swear
fallere deceive, be false
cuius numen di iurare timent et
    fallere by whose power the gods
    fear to swear falsely, *lit.* swear
    and be false

25 cernere see
inops helpless, poor
inhumātus unburied
haec omnis . . . turba

raucus noisy, rumbling
fluentum, n. stream
trānsportāre carry across
nec . . . datur . . . (eos) transportare
    nor is it permitted to carry them
    across
sēdēs, f. *here* = grave
os, n. bone
quiērunt = quiēvērunt: quiēscere
    become still, rest
errāre wander
330 dēmum at last
exoptāre long for
revīsere return to
Anchīsā satus sprung from/son of
    Anchises
vestigium, n. footstep, step
pressit: premere check
sors, f. lot, fate
miserārī pity
iniquus unfair, cruel

7

Caught sight of Italy, being lifted high on a wave crest.
Little by little I swam to the shore. I was all but safe,
When, as I clung to the rough-edged cliff top, my fingers crooked
And my soaking garments weighing me down, some barbarous natives
Attacked me with swords, in their ignorance thinking that I was a rich
    prize.
Now the waves have me, the winds keep tossing me up on the shore
    again.
So now, by the sweet light and breath of heaven above
I implore you, and by your father, by your hopes for growing Ascanius
Redeem me from this doom, unconquered one! Please sprinkle
Dust on my corpse — you can do it and quickly get back to port Velia:
Or else, if way there is, some way that your heavenly mother
Is showing you (not, for sure, without the assent of deity
Would you be going to cross the swampy Stygian stream),
Give poor Palinurus your hand, take me with you across the water
So that at least I may rest in the quiet place, in death.
    Thus did the phantom speak, and the Sibyl began to speak thus: —
    This longing of yours, Palinurus, has carried you quite away.
Shall you, unburied, view the Styx, the austere river
Of the Infernal gods, or come to its bank unbidden?
Give up this hope that the course of fate can be swerved by prayer.
But hear and remember my words, to console you in your hard fortune.
I say that the neighbouring peoples, compelled by portents from heaven
Occurring in every township, shall expiate your death,
Shall give you burial and offer the solemn dues to your grave,
And the place shall keep the name of Palinurus for ever.
    Her sayings eased for a while the anguish of his sad heart;
He forgot his cares in the joy of giving his name to a region.

Ergo iter inceptum peragunt fluvioque propinquant.
navita quos iam inde ut Stygia prospexit ab unda   385
per tacitum nemus ire pedemque advertere ripae,
sic prior adgreditur dictis atque increpat ultro:
'quisquis es, armatus qui nostra ad flumina tendis,
fare age quid venias, iam istinc, et comprime gressum.

384 **peragere** carry through, continue
   propinquāre approach
385 **ut** *here* = when
   nemus, n. grove
   iam ut navita inde ab Stygia unda
      prospexit quos (= *them*) . . . *ire*
   advertere turn towards
   prior first
   adgreditur dictis challenges, *lit.*
      attacks with words
   increpāre rebuke

ultrò of his own accord
quisquis whoever
tendere ad + **Form B (accusative)**
   make for, approach
fāre tell me
age come on!
quid why
istinc from there
comprimere check
gressus, m. step

9

umbrarum hic locus est, somni noctisque soporae: 390
corpora viva nefas Stygia vectare carina.
nec vero Alciden me sum laetatus euntem
accepisse lacu, nec Thesea Pirithoumque,
dis quamquam geniti atque invicti viribus essent.
Tartareum ille manu custodem in vincla petivit   395
ipsius a solio regis traxitque trementem;
hi dominam Ditis thalamo deducere adorti.'
quae contra breviter fata est Amphrysia vates:
'nullae hic insidiae tales (absiste moveri),
nec vim tela ferunt; licet ingens ianitor antro   400
aeternum latrans exsangues terreat umbras,
casta licet patrui servet Proserpina limen.
Troius Aeneas, pietate insignis et armis,
ad genitorem imas Erebi descendit ad umbras.
si te nulla movet tantae pietatis imago,   405
at ramum hunc' (aperit ramum qui veste latebat)
'agnoscas.' tumida ex ira tum corda residunt;
nec plura his. ille admirans venerabile donum
fatalis virgae longo post tempore visum
caeruleam advertit puppim ripaeque propinquat.   410
inde alias animas, quae per iuga longa sedebant,
deturbat laxatque foros; simul accipit alveo
ingentem Aenean. gemuit sub pondere cumba
sutilis et multam accepit rimosa paludem.
tandem trans fluvium incolumes vatemque virumque   415
informi limo glaucaque exponit in ulva.
    Cerberus haec ingens latratu regna trifauci
personat adverso recubans immanis in antro.
cui vates horrere videns iam colla colubris

10

390 somnus, m. sleep
soporus drowsy
nefās, n. crime, wrong
vectāre carry
carina, f. boat
nefas (est) corpora viva (in) Stygia
    carina vectare
vērō indeed
Alcidēs, m. descendant of Alceus,
    Hercules, famed for his labours
laetāri rejoice, be glad
euntem when he came (present
    participle of ire)
nec vero laetatus sum me Alciden
    euntem lacu accepisse
Thēseus, m. Theseus, heroic king of
    Athens
Pīrithous, m. Pirithous, friend of
    Theseus
dīs ... geniti descendants of the
    gods
invictus unconquered
vīs, f. (pl. virēs) force, pl. strength
395 vincla = vincula
in vincla petivit sought (to put) into
    chains
solium, n. throne
trementem a solio regis ipsius traxit
adorti (sunt): adoriri attempt
Amphrȳsia vātēs the Amphrysian
    prophetess, the Sibyl
absistere withdraw, cease
400 tēlum, n. weapon
licēre be permitted, may
iānitor, m. doorkeeper
antrum, n. cave
aeternum for ever
lātrāre bark
exsanguis bloodless, pale
castus chaste, pure
patruus, m. uncle
Prōserpina, f. Proserpina, wife of Dis
licet Proserpina casta limen patrui
    servet
pietās, f. goodness, devotion
insignis outstanding, famous

arma, n.pl. arms, weapons, here =
    skill at arms
genitor, m. father
imus lowest, deepest
Erebus, m. the Underworld
405 imāgō, f. image, sight
aperīre open, disclose
latēre lie hidden
tumidus swelling
cor, n. heart
residere subside
plūs more
venerābilis to be revered, awesome
fātālis fateful
virga, f. rod, branch
410 caeruleus dark blue, dark
puppis, f. stern, boat
iugum, n. yoke, ridge, here =
    rowing-bench
dēturbāre turn out
laxāre make loose, here = clear
forus, m. gangway
alveus, m. hull, boat
gemere groan
pondus, n. weight
sūtilis stitched
rimōsus leaky
415 incolumis safe
infōrmis shapeless
līmus, m. mud
exponit vatemque virumque
    incolumes trans fluvium in
    informi limo
glaucus grey
ulva, f. sedge, rushes
Cerberus, m. Cerberus, the watchdog
    of the Underworld
lātrātus, m. barking
trifaux three-throated
personāre make resound
recubāre lie
immānis huge
horrēre bristle
collum, n. neck
coluber, m. snake

11

melle soporatam et medicatis frugibus offam 420
obicit. ille fame rabida tria guttura pandens
corripit obiectam, atque immania terga resolvit
fusus humi totoque ingens extenditur antro.
occupat Aeneas aditum custode sepulto
evaditque celer ripam inremeabilis undae. 425
  Continuo auditae voces vagitus et ingens
infantumque animae flentes, in limine primo
quos dulcis vitae exsortes et ab ubere raptos
abstulit atra dies et funere mersit acerbo.
hos iuxta falso damnati crimine mortis; 430
nec vero hae sine sorte datae, sine iudice, sedes:
quaesitor Minos urnam movet; ille silentum
consiliumque vocat vitasque et crimina discit.
proxima deinde tenent maesti loca, qui sibi letum
insontes peperere manu lucemque perosi 435
proiecere animas. quam vellent aethere in alto
nunc et pauperiem et duros perferre labores!
fas obstat, tristisque palus inamabilis undae
alligat et novies Styx interfusa coercet.
nec procul hinc partem fusi monstrantur in omnem 440
Lugentes campi; sic illos nomine dicunt.
hic quos durus amor crudeli tabe peredit
secreti celant calles et myrtea circum
silva tegit; curae non ipsa in morte relinquunt.
his Phaedram Procrinque locis maestamque Eriphylen 445
crudelis nati monstrantem vulnera cernit,
Evadnenque et Pasiphaen; his Laodamia
it comes et iuvenis quondam, nunc femina, Caeneus
rursus et in veterem fato revoluta figuram.
inter quas Phoenissa recens a vulnere Dido 450
errabat silva in magna; quam Troius heros
ut primum iuxta stetit agnovitque per umbras
obscuram, qualem primo qui surgere mense
aut videt aut vidisse putat per nubila lunam,

12

420 mel, n. honey
sopŏrātus drowsy, soporific
medicātus drugged
frūgēs, f.pl. corn, grain
offa, f. titbit
obicere throw to
rabidus frenzied
guttur, n. throat
pandere *here* = open
ille . . . corripit (offam) obiectam
tergum, n. back
resolvere unfasten, relax
fūsus: fundere pour out, spread out
sepultus (somnō) buried (in sleep)
425 ēvādere go out, pass beyond
celer swift
inremeābilis not to be crossed again
continuō at once
vāgitus, m. wailing
infāns, m.f. baby
flēre weep
auditae (sunt) voces et vagitus ingens
et flentes animae infantum quos
atra dies abstulit
dulcis sweet, dear
exsors + Form D (genitive) having no
share in
ūber, n. breast
fūnus, n. death
mergere plunge, immerse
acerbus bitter, *here* = untimely
430 iuxtā + Form B (accusative) next to
falsō . . . crimine on a false charge
damnāre mortis condemn to death
iuxta hos (sunt) falso crimine mortis
damnati
iūdex, m. judge
quaesitor, m. inquisitor
Minōs, m. King Minos, judge of the
dead
urna, f. urn, jar
silentēs, m.pl. the silent, the dead
maestus sad, unhappy
435 insōns guiltless
peperēre = peperērunt: parere
produce, bring about

lūcem perōsus hating the light (of
life)
prōiĕcēre = prōiĕcērunt: prōicere
throw away
aethēr, m. upper air, air above
pauperiēs, f. poverty
perferre endure
fās, n. divine law, right
inamābilis unlovely, hateful
alligāre bind round
noviēs nine times
interfūsus flowing between
440 mōnstrāre show, display
lūgēre mourn, grieve
campus, m. field, plain
Lugentes campi in omnem partem
fusi monstrantur
crūdēlis cruel
tābēs, f. wasting away
perēdit: perēsse eat away
sēcrētus set apart, secret
callis, m. path
myrteus of myrtle
tegere cover
secreti calles celant (eos) quos durus
amor . . . peredit
445 Phaedra, f. Phaedra ⎫
Procris, f. Procris ⎪
Eriphȳlē, f. Eriphyle ⎪ all
Ēvadnē, f. Evadne ⎬ victims
Pāsiphaē, f. Pasiphae ⎪ of
Lāodamia, f. Laodamia ⎪ unhappy
Caeneus, m. Caeneus ⎪ love
(formerly a girl, ⎪ affairs
Caenis) ⎭
fātum, n. fate, destiny
revolvere turn back
figūra, f. shape
450 Phoenissus Phoenician
recēns fresh
Didō, f. Dido, queen of Carthage
qualem lunam qui surgere aut videt
aut vidisse putat, like the moon
which someone either sees or
thinks he has seen rising
nūbila, n.pl. clouds

13

demisit lacrimas dulcique adfatus amore est: **455**
'infelix Dido, verus mihi nuntius ergo
venerat exstinctam ferroque extrema secutam?
funeris heu tibi causa fui? per sidera iuro,
per superos et si qua fides tellure sub ima est,
invitus, regina, tuo de litore cessi.   **460**
sed me iussa deum, quae nunc has ire per umbras,
per loca senta situ cogunt noctemque profundam,
imperiis egere suis; nec credere quivi
hunc tantum tibi me discessu ferre dolorem.
siste gradum teque aspectu ne subtrahe nostro.   **465**
quem fugis? extremum fato quod te adloquor hoc est.'
talibus Aeneas ardentem et torva tuentem
lenibat dictis animum lacrimasque ciebat.
illa solo fixos oculos aversa tenebat
nec magis incepto vultum sermone movetur   **470**
quam si dura silex aut stet Marpesia cautes.
tandem corripuit sese atque inimica refugit
in nemus umbriferum, coniunx ubi pristinus illi
respondet curis aequatque Sychaeus amorem.
nec minus Aeneas casu percussus iniquo   **475**
prosequitur lacrimis longe et miseratur euntem.
    Inde datum molitur iter. iamque arva tenebant
ultima, quae bello clari secreta frequentant.
hic illi occurrit Tydeus, hic inclutus armis
Parthenopaeus et Adrasti pallentis imago,   **480**
hic multum fleti ad superos belloque caduci
Dardanidae, quos ille omnes longo ordine cernens
ingemuit, Glaucumque Medontaque Thersilochumque,
tres Antenoridas Cererique sacrum Polyboeten,
Idaeumque etiam currus, etiam arma tenentem.   **485**

455 adfārī speak to, address
exstinguere extinguish, kill
extrēma sequi seek death, *lit.* pursue
last things
verus nuntius mihi venerat (te)
exstinctam (esse) . . . secutam
(esse)
heu = ēheu
sidus, n. constellation, star
superī, m.pl. the gods above
si qua fides tellure sub ima est, by
whatever good faith there is deep   475
below the earth, *lit.* if there is any
good faith beneath deepest earth
460 cēdere depart
sed iussa deum . . . egere . . . me
imperiis suis
sentus rough
situs, m. position, *here* = neglect
profundus deep
imperium, n. dominion, command
quivī: quīre be able
discessus, m. departure   480
me ferre tibi hunc tantum dolorem
465 sistere set, check
gradus, m. step
aspectus, m. sight
subtrahere withdraw
nē subtrahe = nōlī subtrahere
hoc est extremum fato quod, this is
fated to be the last time that, *lit.*
this is the last by fate that
ardēre burn, blaze (with anger)
torva tuentem glaring, *lit.* looking
fierce things
lēnībat = lēniēbat: lēnīre soften,
soothe
ciēre rouse
solum, n. ground
figere fix
āvertere turn away
470 *nec magis . . . movetur . . . quam si*
silex, f. flint
Marpēsius from Marpessus, a mountain on the island of Paros,   485
famous for marble

cautēs, f. rock, crag
sēsē = sē
sē corripere take oneself off, hasten
away
refugere run back
umbrifer shadowy
coniūnx, m. husband
pristinus former
aequāre equal, *here* = return
Sychaeus, m. Sychaeus, once king of
Phoenicia
nec minus nevertheless
cāsus, m. fall, fate
percussus: percutere strike, shatter
prōsequi follow
mōlītur iter he toils along the way
arvum, n. field
clārus famous
occurrere + Form C (dative) run to
meet
inclutus famed, glorious
Tȳdeus, m. Tydeus ⎫ heroes who
Parthenopaeus, m. ⎪ fought in the
Parthenopaeus ⎬ war known as
Adrastus, m. ⎪ Seven against
Adrastus ⎭ Thebes
imāgō, f. ghost
multum flētī ad superōs much
mourned among the living, *lit.*
much wept among those above
cadūcus fallen
Dardanidae, m.pl. Trojans, descendants of Dardanus, founder of the
Trojan race
ingemere groan
Glaucus, m. Glaucus ⎫
Medōn, m. Medon ⎪
Thersilochus, m. ⎪
Thersilochus ⎬ Trojan
Antēnoridae, m.pl. ⎪ heroes
sons of Antenor ⎪
Polyboetēs, m. Polyboetes ⎪
Īdaeus, m. Idaeus ⎭
Cerēs, f. the goddess Ceres
currus, m. chariot   485

circumstant animae dextra laevaque frequentes,
nec vidisse semel satis est; iuvat usque morari
et conferre gradum et veniendi discere causas.
at Danaum proceres Agamemnoniaeque phalanges
ut videre virum fulgentiaque arma per umbras,   490
ingenti trepidare metu; pars vertere terga,
ceu quondam petiere rates, pars tollere vocem
exiguam: inceptus clamor frustratur hiantes.

    Just then Aeneas caught sight of Deiphobus, his whole body   494
A mass of wounds, most horribly mangled about the face —
The face and both the hands, head mutilated with ears
Torn off, and the nose lopped — a barbarous disfigurement.
The moment he'd recognised that shrinking creature who covered
His ghastly wounds, Aeneas burst out in familiar tones: —
    Deiphobus, great fighter, descended from high-born Teucer,
Who was it chose to inflict atrocious punishment on you?
Who could go to such lengths against you? On Troy's last night
I heard a rumour that, worn out with killing and killing Greeks,
You had sunk down on a huge indiscriminate heap of dead bodies.
Then, myself, I erected by the Rhoetean shore
A cenotaph for you, and thrice invoked your spirit aloud.
Your name and a trophy mark the spot; yourself I could not
Find to inter in your native soil before I departed.
    The son of Priam replied: —
                    Dear friend, you neglected nothing;
All that was needed you've done for Deiphobus and his shade.
My destiny and the destructive nature of that Lacaenian
Woman brought me to this: it was she who gave me these souvenirs.
You remember how we spent that last night in rejoicings,
In a fools' paradise; too well, no doubt, you remember it.
When the horse of doom had cleared at a bound the battlements
Of Troy, bearing an armed detachment within its belly,
That woman faked a dance, led the Trojan women around,
Yelling in Bacchanal orgy; under cover of which herself
With a blazing torch in her hand signalled the Greeks from our citadel.
I, worn out by our ordeals and leaden with sleep, was lying
In my unlucky bedroom under a coverlet
Of deep, delicious rest, very like the peace of death.

16

circumstant . . . frequentēs stand round (him) in crowds
dextrā laevāque on the right and left
semel once
nec satis est (eum) vidisse semel 490
iuvat (eōs) it pleases them, they take pleasure in
usque continually, indefinitely, for a long time
cōnferre gradum match their step, walk beside
Danaum = Danaōrum: Danaī, m.pl. the Greeks

procer, m. chief
Agamemnonius of Agamemnon, leader of the Greek army at Troy
phalanx, f. phalanx, battle line
vidēre = vidērunt
trepidāre panic
ceu just as
petiēre = petīvērunt
exiguus small, thin, ghostly
frūstrārī mock, fool
hiāre gape

17

Meantime that nonpareil wife of mine removed all the arms from
Our house, yes, even my trusty sword from beneath my pillow;
Then called Menelaus inside, opened the door to him, hoping —
Vile thing — to make a wonderful present of me to her lover
And thus erase the stigma of her old wicked doings.
No more of this: they burst into the bedroom; Ulysses was with them,
Promoter and compère of crimes. Ye gods, may such deeds recoil
On the Greeks, if my prayer for revenge is made with a clear conscience.
But tell me now, in turn, what chance has brought you here
Alive. Were you compelled by your wanderings on the ocean,
Or a command from heaven? Or what fate irks you, that you should
Enter this joyless, sunless abode, these vague, vexed regions?

So they conversed, till Aurora, driving her rosy chariot,
Had passed the midway point of the sky in her flying course;
And indeed they might have used up all the allotted time thus,
Had not his guide, the Sibyl, spoken a few words of warning: —

Night comes apace, Aeneas; yet we spend the hours in grieving.
Here is the spot where the way forks, going in two directions;
The right-hand leads beneath the battlements of great Dis,
And is our route to Elysium; the left-hand takes the wicked
To Tartarus, their own place, and punishment condign.

Deiphobus said: —
Great Sibyl, do not be angry with me.
I will leave you, return to the shades and make their number complete.
Fare on, Aeneas, our pride, and with better luck than mine!

Thus he spoke, and speaking, turned on his heel and went.

Aeneas looked back on a sudden: he saw to his left a cliff
Overhanging a spread of battlements, a threefold wall about them,
Girdled too by a swift-running stream, a flaming torrent —
Hell's river of fire, whose current rolls clashing rocks along.
In front, an enormous portal, the door-posts columns of adamant,
So strong that no mortal violence nor even the heaven-dwellers
Can broach it: an iron tower stands sheer and soaring above it,
Whereupon Tisiphone sits, wrapped in a bloodstained robe,
Sleeplessly, day-long, night-long, guarding the forecourt there.
From within can be heard the sounds of groaning and brutal lashing,
Sounds of clanking iron, of chains being dragged along.
Scared by the din, Aeneas halted; he could not move: —

What kinds of criminals are these? Speak, lady! What punishments
Afflict them, that such agonised sounds rise up from there?

Then the Sibyl began: —
O famous lord of the Trojans,

18

No righteous soul may tread that threshold of the damned:
But, when Hecate appointed me to the Avernian grove,
She instructed me in heaven's punishments, showed me all.
Here Rhadamanthus rules, and most severe his rule is,
Trying and chastising wrongdoers, forcing confessions
From any who, on earth, went gleefully undetected —
But uselessly, since they have only postponed till death their atonement.
At once Tisiphone, the avenger, scourge in hand,
Pounces upon the guilty, lashing them, threatening them
With the angry snakes in her left hand, and calls up her bloodthirsty
     sisters.
Then at last the hinges screech, the infernal gates
Grind open. Do you see the sentry, who she is,
Posted over the forecourt? the shape that guards the threshold?
Within, there dwells a thing more fierce — the fifty-headed
Hydra, with all its black throats agape. Then Tartarus
Goes sheer down under the shades, an abyss double in depth
The height that Olympus stands above a man gazing skyward.
Here Earth's primaeval offspring, the breed of Titans, who
Were hurled down by Jove's lightning, writhe in the bottomless pit.
Here have I seen the twin sons of Aloeus, the gigantic
Creatures who sought to pull down heaven itself with their own
Bare hands, and to unseat Jove from his throne above.
Salmoneus too have I seen undergoing the rigorous sentence
Imposed when he mimicked the thunder and lightning of Jove almighty:
Drawn by a four-horse team and shaking a lighted torch,
He would go through Greece exulting, even through the middle of Elis
City, claiming the homage due to the gods alone —
Madman, to copy the nonpareil lightning, the thunderstorm
With a rumble of bronze wheels and a clatter of hard-hoofed horses!
But the Father almighty, among his serried storm clouds, launched
A weapon — no torches, no smoky light of farthing dips
Was this — and hurled the blasphemer down with the wind of its
     passage.
Tityos too, the nursling of Earth who mothers all,
Was to be seen, his body pegged out over a full nine
Acres, a huge vulture with hooked beak gnawing for ever
His inexhaustible liver, the guts that are rich in torment,
Pecking away for its food, burrowing deep in the body
It lives in, and giving no rest to the always-replenished vitals.
Need I mention the Lapithae, Ixion or Pirithous?
Over them, always about to fall and looking as if it were

Falling, a black crag hangs: banqueting couches gleam with
Golden legs, raised high, and feasts of regal opulence
Are set before damned eyes; but the chief of the Furies, reclining
Nearby, forbids them to stretch out their hands for the food; she leaps
 up,
Menacing them with her lifted torch, and shouts like thunder.
Here are those who in life hated their own brothers,
Or struck their parents; those who entangled their dependants
In fraudulent dealing; and those who sat tight on the wealth they had
 won,
Setting none aside for their own kin — most numerous of all are these;
Then such as were killed for adultery, took part in militant treason,
Men who made bold to break faith with their masters: — all such await
Punishment, mewed up here. And seek not to know what punishment,
What kind of destined torment awaits each one in the Pit.
Some have to roll huge rocks; some whirl round, spreadeagled
On spokes of wheels: the tragic Theseus sits, condemned to
Spend eternity in that chair: the poor wretch, Phlegyas,
Admonishes all, crying out through the mirk in solemn avowal,
"Be warned by me! Learn justice, and not to belittle the gods!"
One sold his country for gold, putting her under the yoke of
Dictatorship, and corruptly made and unmade her laws;
One entered the bed of his daughter, forced an unholy mating:
All dared some abominable thing, and what they dared they did.
No, not if I had a hundred tongues, a hundred mouths
And a voice of iron, could I describe all the shapes of wickedness,
Catalogue all the retributions inflicted here.

 Haec ubi dicta dedit Phoebi longaeva sacerdos,
'sed iam age, carpe viam et susceptum perfice munus;
acceleremus' ait; 'Cyclopum educta caminis   630
moenia conspicio atque adverso fornice portas,
haec ubi nos praecepta iubent deponere dona.'
dixerat et pariter gressi per opaca viarum
corripiunt spatium medium foribusque propinquant.
occupat Aeneas aditum corpusque recenti   635
spargit aqua ramumque adverso in limine figit.
 His demum exactis, perfecto munere divae,
devenere locos laetos et amoena virecta

628 **Phoebus, m.** the god Apollo
carpere pick, *here* take up, continue
mŭnus, n. gift, duty, task
630 **accelerāre** hurry, hasten
Cÿclōpes, m.pl. the Cyclopes, a race
of one-eyed giants
ēdūcere draw out, forge
caminus m. furnace
moenia, n.pl. walls
fornix, m. arch
praeceptum, n. order, command
*ubi praecepta iubent nos deponere
haec dona*
pariter alike, side by side

gressus: gradi step, walk
per opāca viārum along the
shadowed roads
corripere *here* = hasten across
spatium medium the space between,
lit. the middle space
636 **spargere** sprinkle
exāctus: exigere complete
dĭva, f. goddess
dēvēnēre = dēvēnērunt: dēvenire
come down to
amoenus lovely, pleasant
virēcta, n.pl. green places, lawns

21

fortunatorum nemorum sedesque beatas.
largior hic campos aether et lumine vestit   640
purpureo, solemque suum, sua sidera norunt.
pars in gramineis exercent membra palaestris,
contendunt ludo et fulva luctantur harena;
pars pedibus plaudunt choreas et carmina dicunt.
nec non Threicius longa cum veste sacerdos   645
obloquitur numeris septem discrimina vocum,
iamque eadem digitis, iam pectine pulsat eburno.
hic genus antiquum Teucri, pulcherrima proles,
magnanimi heroes nati melioribus annis,
Ilusque Assaracusque et Troiae Dardanus auctor.   650
arma procul currusque virum miratur inanes;
stant terra defixae hastae passimque soluti
per campum pascuntur equi. quae gratia currum
armorumque fuit vivis, quae cura nitentes
pascere equos, eadem sequitur tellure repostos.   655
conspicit, ecce, alios dextra laevaque per herbam
vescentes laetumque choro paeana canentes
inter odoratum lauris nemus, unde superne
plurimus Eridani per silvam volvitur amnis.
hic manus ob patriam pugnando vulnera passi,   660
quique sacerdotes casti, dum vita manebat,
quique pii vates et Phoebo digna locuti,
inventas aut qui vitam excoluere per artes
quique sui memores aliquos fecere merendo:
omnibus his nivea cinguntur tempora vitta.   665

Now the Sibyl addressed the company dotted about there,   666
And specially Musaeus, for round him was a large group
Gazing up at him as he towered head and shoulders above them: —
    Tell me, you blessed spirits, and you, most honoured poet,
Whereabouts can we find Anchises? We have come here,
Crossing the great rivers of the Underworld, to see him.
    So did Musaeus make reply with these few words: —
None of us has a fixed abode: we dwell in shady

22

beātus fortunate, blessed
640 largus spacious, generous
vestīre clothe
purpureus bright
hic aether largior et lumine purpureo
campos vestit
nōrunt = nōvērunt: nōscere get to
know, *perfect* = know
grāmineus grassy
membrum, n. limb
palaestra, f. wrestling-ground
contendere compete
lūdus, m. game, sport
fulvus tawny, yellow
luctārī wrestle
plaudere beat out, tread
chorēa (*here* chorea), f. dance
carmen, n. song
645 nec nōn and also
Thrēicius . . . sacerdōs the Thracian
priest, Orpheus
obloquī play as an accompaniment
numerus, m. number, rhythm
discrīmina vōcum different notes
digitus, m. finger
pecten, m. plectrum
ebūrnus ivory
iamque eadem (discrimina) digitis
pulsat, iam pectine eburno
genus, n. race
antīquus ancient
Teucer, m. Teucer, ancestor of the
Trojans
nātī: nāscī be born
50 Īlus, m. Ilus, grandfather of Priam
Assaracus, m. Assaracus, grandfather
of Anchises
Dardanus, m. Dardanus, founder of
Troy
hasta, f. spear

passim everywhere, here and there
solūtī: solvere release, unharness
pāscere feed; *passive* = graze
grātia, f. pleasure
nitēns shining, glossy
655 repostōs = repositōs: repōnere
lay to rest
gratia quae curr(u)um armorumque
fuit (eis) vivis, quae cura . . .
eadem (gratia, eadem cura)
sequitur (eos) tellure repostos
herba, f. grass
vescī feed, feast
chorus, m. choir
paeān, m. hymn of praise
canere sing
odōrātus scented, fragrant
laurus, f. laurel
supernē from above
Ēridanus, m. the river Eridanus
660 manus, f. *here* = band of men
hic (est) manus (eorum qui) . . .
vulnera passi (sunt)
ob for
patria, f. fatherland, native country
pius good, dutiful, holy
dignus + Form E (ablative) worthy
of
quique (erant) pii vates et (verba)
Phoebo digna locuti (sunt)
excoluēre = excoluērunt: excolere
improve, enhance
per artes inventas through the skills
they discovered
fēcēre = fēcērunt
merēre deserve
665 niveus snow-white
cingere surround, encircle
tempora, n.pl. temples (of the head),
brow

Groves, we make our beds on river-banks, reside in
Watersweet meadows. But if your heart's desire is such,
Then climb this rise and I'll set your feet on an easy path.
    He spoke, and leading the way, showed them the luminous plains
Extending below them. Now they went down from the upland heights.

    At pater Anchises penitus convalle virenti
inclusas animas superumque ad lumen ituras   680
lustrabat studio recolens, omnemque suorum
forte recensebat numerum, carosque nepotes
fataque fortunasque virum moresque manusque.
isque ubi tendentem adversum per gramina vidit
Aenean, alacres palmas utrasque tetendit,   685
effusaeque genis lacrimae et vox excidit ore:
'venisti tandem, tuaque exspectata parenti
vicit iter durum pietas? datur ora tueri,
nate, tua et notas audire et reddere voces?
sic equidem ducebam animo rebarque futurum   690
tempora dinumerans, nec me mea cura fefellit.
quas ego te terras et quanta per aequora vectum
accipio! quantis iactatum, nate, periclis!
quam metui ne quid Libyae tibi regna nocerent!'
ille autem: 'tua me, genitor, tua tristis imago   695
saepius occurrens haec limina tendere adegit;
stant sale Tyrrheno classes. da iungere dextram,
da, genitor, teque amplexu ne subtrahe nostro.'
sic memorans largo fletu simul ora rigabat.
ter conatus ibi collo dare bracchia circum;   700
ter frustra comprensa manus effugit imago,
par levibus ventis volucrique simillima somno.
    Interea videt Aeneas in valle reducta
seclusum nemus et virgulta sonantia silvae,
Lethaeumque domos placidas qui praenatat amnem.   705

24

679 penitus + Form E (ablative) deep in
convallis, f. valley
virēns green
680 inclūdere enclose, confine
itūrus *future participle of ire*
destined to go
lūstrāre survey
studiō recolēns earnestly contem-
plating
recēnsēre review
cārus dear
nepōs, m. grandson, descendant
virum = virōrum
manūs, f.pl. *here* = works of their
hands, handiwork
grāmen, n. grass
685 alacer eager
uterque both
effusae . . . (*sunt*)
gena, f. cheek
vōx, f. *here* = words
excidere fall from, tumble out
tua exspectāta parentī . . . pietās the
loving duty your father expected,
lit. your expected duty to your
parent
tuērī behold
690 equidem indeed
dūcere *here* = reckon
rērī think
rebar (*id*) *futurum* (*esse*)
dīnumerāre calculate
quas . . . *terras et per quanta aequora
te vectum accipio!* over what
lands and what great seas you
have travelled before I welcome
you now, *lit.* I welcome you

having travelled over what
lands . . .
iactāre toss
pericla = pericula
metuere fear
quid in some way
Libya, f. *here* = North Africa, where
Dido had founded the city of
Carthage
695 *ille autem* (*respondit*)
adigere drive, urge
sale Tyrrhēnō on the Tyrrhenian sea
da (*mihi*) *iungere* let me grasp, *lit.*
join
amplexus, m. embrace
memorāre speak, speak of
flētus, m. weeping, tears
rigāre wet
700 ter three times
circum . . . dare + Form C (dative)
put round
comprēnsa = comprehēnsa: comprehendere grasp
*ter imago frustra comprensa manus
effugit*
levis light
ventus, m. wind
volucer winged
vallis, f. valley
reductus withdrawn, remote
sēclūsus secluded
virgulta, n.pl. thickets, undergrowth
sonāre resound, rustle
705 placidus peaceful
praenatāre flow past
*amnem Lethaeum qui domos placidas
praenatat*

hunc circum innumerae gentes populique volabant:
ac veluti in pratis ubi apes aestate serena
floribus insidunt variis et candida circum
lilia funduntur, strepit omnis murmure campus.
horrescit visu subito causasque requirit   710
inscius Aeneas, quae sint ea flumina porro,
quive viri tanto complerint agmine ripas.
tum pater Anchises: 'animae, quibus altera fato
corpora debentur, Lethaei ad fluminis undam
securos latices et longa oblivia potant.   715
has equidem memorare tibi atque ostendere coram
iampridem, hanc prolem cupio enumerare meorum,
quo magis Italia mecum laetere reperta.'

But, father, must it be deemed that some souls ascend from here 719
To our earthly scene? re-enter our dull corporeal existence?
Why ever should so perverse a craving for earth possess them?
　　I will tell you, my son, certainly; I will not keep you in doubt,
　　Answered Anchises, and then enlarged on each point successively: —
　　First, you must know that the heavens, the earth, the watery plains
Of the sea, the moon's bright globe, the sun and the stars are all
Sustained by a spirit within; for immanent Mind, flowing
Through all its parts and leavening its mass, makes the universe work.
This union produced mankind, the beasts, the birds of the air,
And the strange creatures that live under the sea's smooth face.
The life-force of those seeds is fire, their source celestial,
But they are deadened and dimmed by the sinful bodies they live in —
The flesh that is laden with death, the anatomy of clay:
Whence these souls of ours feel fear, desire, grief, joy,
But encased in their blind, dark prison discern not the heaven-light
　　above.
Yes, not even when the last flicker of life has left us,
Does evil, or the ills that flesh is heir to, quite
Relinquish our souls; it must be that many a taint grows deeply,
Mysteriously grained in their being from long contact with the body.
Therefore the dead are disciplined in purgatory, and pay
The penalty of old evil: some hang, stretched to the blast of
Vacuum winds; for others, the stain of sin is washed
Away in a vast whirlpool or cauterised with fire.

26

innumerus countless
velutī = velut   715
prātum, n. meadow
apis, f. bee
insidere + Form C (dative) settle on
candidus bright, white
strepere hum
murmur, n. murmuring, buzzing
10 horrēscere shudder
visus, m. sight
requīrere ask
porrō far off, at a distance
complērint = complēvērint: complēre
   fill

agmen, n. crowd, band
sēcūrōs laticēs care-dispelling waters
oblīvia, n.pl. forgetfulness
pōtāre drink
equidem cupio has memorare tibi
cōram face to face
iampridem for a long time now
ēnumerāre count over
quō magis so that . . . all the more
laetēre = laetēris
reperīre discover

Each of us finds in the next world his own level: a few of us
Are later released to wander at will through broad Elysium,
The Happy Fields; until, in the fullness of time, the ages
Have purged that ingrown stain, and nothing is left but pure
Ethereal sentience and the spirit's essential flame.
All these souls, when they have finished their thousand-year cycle,
God sends for, and they come in crowds to the river of Lethe,
So that, you see, with memory washed out, they may revisit
The earth above and begin to wish to be born again.
 When Anchises had finished, he drew his son and the Sibyl
Into the thick of the murmuring concourse assembled there
And took his stand on an eminence from which he could scan the long
    files
Over against him, and mark the features of those who passed.
 Listen, for I will show you your destiny, setting forth
The fame that from now shall attend the seed of Dardanus,
The posterity that awaits you from an Italian marriage —
Illustrious souls, one day to come in for our Trojan name.
That young man there — do you see him? who leans on an untipped
    spear,
Has been allotted the next passage to life, and first of
All these will ascend to earth, with Italian blood in his veins;
He is Silvius, an Alban name, and destined to be your last child,
The child of your late old age by a wife, Lavinia, who shall
Bear him in sylvan surroundings, a king and the father of kings
Through whom our lineage shall rule in Alba Longa.
Next to him stands Procas, a glory to the Trojan line;
Then Capys and Numitor, and one who'll revive your own name —
Silvius Aeneas, outstanding alike for moral rectitude
And prowess in war, if ever he comes to the Alban throne.
What fine young men they are! Look at their stalwart bearing,
The oak leaves that shade their brows — decorations for saving life!
These shall found your Nomentum, Gabii and Fidenae,
These shall rear on the hills Collatia's citadel,
Pometii, and the Fort of Inuus, Bola and Cora —
All nameless sites at present, but then they shall have these names.
Further, a child of Mars shall go to join his grandsire —
Romulus, born of the stock of Assaracus by his mother,
Ilia. Look at the twin plumes upon his helmet's crest,
Mars' cognisance, which marks him out for the world of earth!
His are the auguries, my son, whereby great Rome

Shall rule to the ends of the earth, shall aspire to the highest achieve-
    ment,
Shall ring the seven hills with a wall to make one city,
Blessed in her breed of men: as Cybele, wearing her turreted
Crown, is charioted round the Phrygian cities, proud of
Her brood of gods, embracing a hundred of her children's children —
Heaven-dwellers all, all tenants of the realm above.
Now bend your gaze this way, look at that people there!
They are *your* Romans. Caesar is there and all Ascanius'
Posterity, who shall pass beneath the arch of day.

hic vir, hic est, tibi quem promitti saepius audis,
Augustus Caesar, divi genus, aurea condet
saecula qui rursus Latio regnata per arva
Saturno quondam, super et Garamantas et Indos
proferet imperium; iacet extra sidera tellus,   795
extra anni solisque vias, ubi caelifer Atlas
axem umero torquet stellis ardentibus aptum.
huius in adventum iam nunc et Caspia regna
responsis horrent divum et Maeotia tellus,
et septemgemini turbant trepida ostia Nili.   800
nec vero Alcides tantum telluris obivit,
fixerit aeripedem cervam licet, aut Erymanthi
pacarit nemora et Lernam tremefecerit arcu;
nec qui pampineis victor iuga flectit habenis
Liber, agens celso Nysae de vertice tigres.   805
et dubitamus adhuc virtutem extendere factis,
aut metus Ausonia prohibet consistere terra?

*Anchises shows Aeneas the spirits of the early kings of Rome and then
the man who drove out the last of them.*

vis et Tarquinios reges animamque superbam
ultoris Bruti, fascesque videre receptos?
consulis imperium hic primus saevasque secures
accipiet, natosque pater nova bella moventes   820
ad poenam pulchra pro libertate vocabit,
infelix, utcumque ferent ea facta minores:
vincet amor patriae laudumque immensa cupido.

792 **Augustus Caesar, m.** the emperor
   Augustus Caesar
   genus, n. *here* = descendant,
   offspring
   condere found, establish
   saeculum, n. generation, age
   rĕgnāre rule
   Sāturnus, m. the god Saturn, who
   ruled Latium in the Golden Age
   qui aurea saecula (in) Latio rursus
   condet per arva quondam (a)
   Saturno regnata
   Garamantes, m.pl. Garamantes, a
   people of North Africa
   Indī, m.pl. Indians
795 **prōferre** extend
   extrā + Form B (accusative) outside,
   beyond
   caelifer sky-bearing
   Atlās, m. the giant Atlas who held
   up the sky
   axis, m. axis, *here* = vault of heaven
   torquēre twist, turn
   stĕlla, f. star
   aptus fitted, inset
   Caspius Caspian
   dīvum = dīvōrum
   Maeōtia tellūs Maeotian land,
   Scythia
800 **septemgeminus** sevenfold

turbāre *here* = be in confusion
ŏstium, n. door, *here* = mouth of
   river
Nīlus, m. the river Nile
aeripēs brazen-footed
cerva, f. deer
licet although
Erymanthus, m. Erymanthus, a
   mountain range in Greece
pācārit = pācāverit: pācāre tame,
   pacify
Lerna, f. Lerna, near Argos, where
   Hercules killed the Hydra
tremefacere make tremble
arcus, m. bow
pampineus of vine tendrils
victor victorious
flectere bend, turn
iuga flectit drives his chariot
habēna, f. rein
805 **Liber, m.** the god Liber, also known
   as Bacchus or Dionysus
nec Liber qui victor iuga pampineis
   habenis flectit
celsus lofty
Nȳsa, f. Mount Nysa
vertex, m. top, summit
tigris, m.f. tiger
factum, n. deed
Ausonia, f. Italy

817 **Tarquinius, m.** Tarquin, name of two
   kings of Rome
   superbus proud
   Brūtus, m. Brutus, who led the
   revolt against the last king of
   Rome
   fascēs, m.pl. fasces, bundles of rods
   symbolising political power
   recipere recover

secūris, f. axe, symbolising power of
   life and death
820 **nova bella moventēs** stirring up fresh
   wars
utcumque however
minōrēs, m.pl. descendants
laus, f. praise
immēnsus immeasurable, great
cupīdō, f. desire

illae autem paribus quas fulgere cernis in armis,
concordes animae nunc et dum nocte prementur,
heu quantum inter se bellum, si lumina vitae
attigerint, quantas acies stragemque ciebunt,
aggeribus socer Alpinis atque arce Monoeci   830
descendens, gener adversis instructus Eois!
ne, pueri, ne tanta animis adsuescite bella
neu patriae validas in viscera vertite vires;
tuque prior, tu parce, genus qui ducis Olympo,
proice tela manu, sanguis meus! —   835

quis te, magne Cato, tacitum aut te, Cosse, relinquat?   841
quis Gracchi genus aut geminos, duo fulmina belli,
Scipiadas, cladem Libyae, parvoque potentem
Fabricium vel te sulco, Serrane, serentem?
quo fessum rapitis, Fabii? tu Maximus ille es,   845
unus qui nobis cunctando restituis rem.
excudent alii spirantia mollius aera
(credo equidem), vivos ducent de marmore vultus,
orabunt causas melius, caelique meatus
describent radio et surgentia sidera dicent: 850
tu regere imperio populos, Romane, memento
(hae tibi erunt artes), pacique imponere morem,
parcere subiectis et debellare superbos.'

They marvelled at Anchises' words, and he went on: —   854
    Look how Marcellus comes all glorious with the highest
Of trophies, a victor over-topping all other men!
He shall buttress the Roman cause when a great war shakes it,
Shatter the Carthaginian and rebel Gaul with his cavalry,
Give to Quirinus the third set of arms won in single combat.
    Aeneas interposed, seeing beside Marcellus
A youth of fine appearance, in glittering accoutrements,
But his face was far from cheerful and downcast were his eyes: —
    Father, who is he that walks with Marcellus there?
His son? Or one of the noble line of his children's children?

827 concors in harmony
  premere press, weigh down
  illae autem animae quas fulgere in
    paribus armis cernis (*sunt*)
    concordes nunc
  attingere touch, reach
  stragēs, f. slaughter
830 aggeribus . . . Alpinis the Alpine
    ranges
  socer, m. father-in-law (here refers
    to Julius Caesar)
  arx Monoeci, f. Monaco
  gener, m. son-in-law (here refers to
    Pompey the Great)
  Eōus of the East, eastern
  adversis instructus Eōis armed with
    the opposing forces of the East,
    lit. drawn up with opposing
    eastern (forces)
  adsuēscere accustom
  neu = nēve and . . . not, nor
  validus strong
  viscera, n.pl. flesh and blood, heart
  Olympus, m. Mount Olympus, home
    of the gods
  sanguis, m. blood, *here* = descendant,
    son
841 tacitus *here* = unmentioned
  Catō, m. Cato ⎫
  Cossus, m. Cossus ⎪
  Gracchi genus sons of famous
    Gracchus, the   Roman
    Gracchus brothers ⎬ statesmen
  Scipiadae, m.pl.   and
    the Scipios   generals
  Fābricius, m. Fabricius ⎪
  Serrānus, m. Serranus ⎭

fulmen, n. thunderbolt
clādēs, f. destruction, scourge
parvō potentem poor but powerful,
  lit. powerful with little
sulcus, m. furrow
serere sow
845 fessus weary
  quo (*me*) *fessum rapitis . . . ?*
  Fabii, m.pl. the Fabii, a distinguished
    Roman family
  Maximus, m. Quintus Fabius
    Maximus Cunctator, the most
    famous of the family; he wore out
    Hannibal and his invading army
    by his delaying tactics
  cūnctāri delay
  restituere restore
  excūdere forge
  spirāns breathing, lifelike
  molliter softly, smoothly
  aes, n. bronze
  marmor, n. marble
  ōrāre causās plead cases (i.e. in
    court)
  meātus, m. movement
  dēscrībere describe, trace
850 radius, m. measuring-rod
  regere rule
  mementō: *imperative from*
    meminisse remember
  subicere conquer
  dēbellāre subdue

33

How the retinue murmurs around him! How fine is the young man's
     presence!
Yet is his head haloed by sombre shade of night.
     Then father Anchises began, tears welling up in his eyes: —
     My son, do not probe into the sorrows of your kin.
Fate shall allow the earth one glimpse of this young man —
One glimpse, no more. Too puissant had been Rome's stock, ye gods,
In your sight, had such gifts been granted it to keep.
What lamentations of men shall the Campus Martius echo
To Mars' great city! O Tiber, what obsequies you shall see
One day as you glide past the new-built mausoleum!
No lad of the Trojan line shall with such hopeful promise
Exalt his Latin forebears, nor shall the land of Romulus
Ever again be so proud of one she has given birth to.
Alas for the sense of duty, the old-time honour! Alas for
The hand unvanquished in war! Him would no foe have met
In battle and not rued it, whether he charged on foot
Or drove his lathering steed with spurs against the enemy.
Alas, poor youth! If only you could escape your harsh fate!
Marcellus you shall be. Give me armfuls of lilies
That I may scatter their shining blooms and shower these gifts
At least upon the dear soul, all to no purpose though
Such kindness be.

          sic tota passim regione vagantur
aëris in campis latis atque omnia lustrant.
quae postquam Anchises natum per singula duxit
incenditque animum famae venientis amore,
exim bella viro memorat quae deinde gerenda,   890
Laurentesque docet populos urbemque Latini,
et quo quemque modo fugiatque feratque laborem.
     Sunt geminae Somni portae, quarum altera fertur
cornea, qua veris facilis datur exitus umbris,
altera candenti perfecta nitens elephanto,   895
sed falsa ad caelum mittunt insomnia Manes.
his ibi tum natum Anchises unaque Sibyllam
prosequitur dictis portaque emittit eburna.
ille viam secat ad naves sociosque revisit.

36 vagārī wander
āēr, n. air
lātus wide
per singula through everything
)0 exim = exinde then, after that
Laurentēs, m.pl. Laurentians, an
Italian tribe
Latīnus, m. Latinus, king of Latium
quomodo laborem quemque
fugiatque feratque
fertur (esse) is said to be

corneus made of horn
exitus, m. way out
895 candēns white, gleaming
elephantus, m. *here* = ivory
insomnium, n. dream
Mānēs, m.pl. spirits of the dead
ūnā together
ēmittere send out
viam secat makes his way
socius, m. companion

35

Tum se ad Caietae recto fert limite portum.   900
ancora de prora iacitur; stant litore puppes.

900 sē . . . fert he makes his way
      Caiēta, f. Caieta, town on west coast
         of Italy
      rēctus direct

līmes, m. path, course
ancora, f. anchor
prōra, f. prow
iacere throw

VOCABULARY

A

ā, ab + Form E (ablative) — by, from
absistere — cease, withdraw: absistit,
    abstitit
abstulit — see auferre
ac — and
accelerāre — hurry, hasten: accelerat,
    accelerāvit, accelerātus
accipere — receive, welcome: accipit,
    accēpit, acceptus
acerbus, acerba, acerbum — bitter,
    untimely
Acherōn, Acherontis, m. — the
    Acheron, one of the seven rivers
    of the Underworld
aciēs, aciēī, f. — edge, blade, battle line
ad + Form B (accusative) — to, towards
adfari — address, speak to: adfātur,
    adfātus est
adgredī — attack, challenge: adgreditur,
    adgressus est
adhūc — still
adigere — drive, urge: adigit, adēgit,
    adāctus
aditus, aditūs, m. — entrance
adloquī — speak to, address:
    adloquitur, adlocūtus est
admīrārī — wonder at: admīrātur,
    admīrātus est
admittere — admit, allow in: admittit,
    admīsit, admissus
admonēre — warn: admonet, admonuit,
    admonitus
adorīrī — attempt: adoritur, adortus est
Adrastus, Adrastī, m. — Adrastus, a
    hero who fought in the war
    known as Seven against Thebes

adsuēscere — accustom: adsuēscit,
    adsuēvit, adsuētus
adventus, adventūs, m. — coming
adversus, adversa, adversum — facing,
    opposite, opposing
advertere — turn towards, turn against:
    advertit, advertit, adversus
Aenēās, Aenēae, m. — Aeneas
aequāre — equal, match: aequat,
    aequāvit, aequātus
aequor, aequoris, n. — sea
āēr, āeris, m. — air
aeripēs — brazen-footed: aeripedis
aes, aeris, n. — bronze
aestās, aestātis, f. — summer
aestuāre — boil, seethe: aestuat,
    aestuāvit
aeternus, aeterna, aeternum — ever-
    lasting, eternal
aethēr, aetheris, m. — heaven, upper
    air, air
Agamemnonius, Agamemnonia,
    Agamemnonium — of
    Agamemnon, leader of the
    Greek army at Troy
agere — do, drive: agit, ēgit, āctus
age — come on!
agger, aggeris, m. — mound, mountain
    range
agmen, agminis, n. — crowd, band
agnōscere — recognise: agnōscit,
    agnōvit, agnitus
ait — he/she says/said
alacer, alacris, alacre — brisk, eager
Alcīdes, Alcīdae, m. — descendant of
    Alceus, Hercules, famed for his
    Labours

aliquis, aliquid — some, someone,
    something: alicuius
alius, alia, aliud — other, another: alius
alligāre — bind round, restrain: alligat,
    alligāvit, alligātus
Alpīnus, Alpīna, Alpīnum — Alpine
alter, altera, alterum — the other,
    another: alterīus
altus, alta, altum — high, lofty, deep
alveus, alveī, m. — hull, boat
amictus, amictūs, m. — cloak
amnis, amnis, m. — river
amoenus, amoena, amoenum —
    pleasant, lovely
amor, amōris, m. — love
Amphrȳsius, Amphrȳsia, Amphrȳsium
    — Amphrysian
amplexus, amplexūs, m. — embrace
Anchīsēs, Anchīsae, m. — Anchises,
    father of Aeneas
ancora, ancorae, f. — anchor
anima, animae, f. — soul, spirit
animus, animī, m. — mind, heart
annōsus, annōsa, annōsum — aged, full
    of years
annus, annī, m. — year
ante + Form B (accusative) — before
Antēnoridae, Antēnoridārum, m.pl. —
    sons of Antenor
antīquus, antīqua, antīquum — ancient,
    former
antrum, antrī, n. — cave
aperīre — open, disclose: aperit,
    aperuit, apertus
apis, apis, f. — bee
aprīcus, aprīca, aprīcum — sunny
aptus, apta, aptum — fitted, studded,
    inset
aqua, aquae, f. — water
arcēre + Form E (ablative) — keep
    away from: arcet, arcuit
arcus, arcūs, m. — bow
ardēre — burn, blaze: ardet, arsit
arma, armōrum, n.pl. — arms, weapons
armāre — arm: armat, armāvit, armātus
ars, artis, f. — art, skill

arvum, arvī, n. — field
arx, arcis, f. — citadel
    arx Monoecī, f. — Monaco
aspectus, aspectūs, m. — sight
Assaracus, Assaracī, m. — Assaracus,
    grandfather of Anchises
ast = at
at — but
āter, ātra, ātrum — black
Atlās, Atlantis, m. — the giant Atlas
    who held up the sky
atque — and
attingere — reach, touch: attingit,
    attigit, attāctus
auctor, auctōris, m. — founder
audīre — hear, listen to: audit, audīvit,
    audītus
auferre — take away, remove: aufert,
    abstulit, ablātus
Augustus, Augustī, m. — the emperor
    Augustus Caesar
aureus, aurea, aureum — of gold,
    golden
Ausonia, Ausoniae, f. — Italy
aut — or
    aut ... aut — either ... or
autem — but
autumnus, autumnī, m. — autumn
āvertere — turn away: āvertit, āvertit,
    āversus
avis, avis, f. — bird
axis, axis, m. — axis, vault of heaven

B
beātus, beāta, beātum — blessed,
    fortunate
bellum, bellī, n. — war
bēlua, bēluae, f. — beast
bene — well
    melius — better
bifōrmis, bifōrmis, bifōrme — of two
    shapes
bonus, bona, bonum — good
    melior, melior, melius — better
bracchium, bracchiī, n. — arm
breviter — briefly

39

Briareus, Briareī, m. − Briareus, a giant
with a hundred arms
Brūtus, Brūtī, m. − Brutus, who led
the revolt against the last king
of Rome

C

cadere − fall: cadit, cecidit, (cāsūrus)
cadūcus, cadūca, cadūcum − fallen
caelifer, caelifera, caeliferum − heaven-
bearing, sky-bearing
caelum, caelī, n. − sky, heaven
Caeneus, Caeneos, m. − Caeneus,
formerly a girl, Caenis
caenum, caenī, n. − mud
caeruleus, caerulea, caeruleum − dark
blue, dark
Caesar, Caesaris, m. − the emperor
Augustus Caesar
Caiēta, Caiētae, f. − Caieta, town on
west coast of Italy
callis, callis, m. − path
camīnus, camīnī, m. − forge, furnace
campus, campī, m. − plain, field
candēns − white, gleaming: candentis
candidus, candida, candidum − bright,
white
canere − sing: canit, cecinit, cantus
cānitiēs, cānitiēī, f. − whiteness, white
or grey hair
carīna, carīnae, f. − keel, boat
carmen, carminis, n. − song
carpere − pick, take: carpit, carpsit,
carptus
cārus, cāra, cārum − dear
Caspius, Caspia, Caspium − Caspian
castus, casta, castum − chaste, pure,
holy
cāsus, cāsūs, m. − fall, fate
Catō, Catōnis, m. − Cato, a famous
Roman statesman
causa, causae, f. − cause, reason, case
cautēs, cautis, f. − crag, rock
cavus, cava, cavum − hollow
cēdere − yield, depart: cēdit, cessit,
cessus

cēlāre − hide, conceal: cēlat, cēlāvit,
cēlātus
celer, celeris, celere − quick, swift
celsus, celsa, celsum − lofty
Centaurus, Centaurī, m. − the Centaur,
half man and half horse
centum − a hundred
centumgeminus, centumgemina,
centumgeminum − hundredfold
Cerberus, Cerberī, m. − Cerberus, the
watchdog of the Underworld
Cerēs, Cereris, f. − the goddess Ceres
cernere − see: cernit, crēvit, crētus
certus, certa, certum − certain,
definite, true
cerva, cervae, f. − deer
ceu − just as, as if
Charōn, Charontis, m. − Charon, ferryman of the dead
Chimaera, Chimaerae, f. − the
Chimaera, a fire-breathing
monster, part lion, part goat,
part snake
chorēa, chorēae, f. − dance
chorus, chorī, m. − chorus, choir
ciēre − set in motion, rouse: ciet, cīvit,
citus
cingere − surround, encircle: cingit,
cīnxit, cīnctus
circum + Form B (accusative) −
around
circumdare − put round: circumdat,
circumdedit, circumdatus
circumstāre − stand round: circumstat,
circumstetit
clādēs, clādis, f. − disaster, destruction,
scourge
clāmor, clāmōris, m. − shout, war-cry
clārus, clāra, clārum − famous
classis, classis, f. − fleet
Cōcȳtus, Cōcȳtī, m. − the river
Cocytus in the Underworld
coercēre − keep together, confine:
coercet, coercuit, coercitus
cōgere − compel, force: cōgit, coēgit,
coāctus

collum, collī, n. — neck
color, colōris, m. — colour
coluber, colubrī, m. — snake
comes, comitis, m.f. — companion
complēre — fill: complet, complēvit,
    complētus
comprehendere — grasp:
    comprehendit, comprehendit,
    comprehēnsus
comprimere — compress, check:
    comprimit, compressit,
    compressus
cōnārī — try: cōnātur, cōnātus est
concors — agreeing, in harmony:
    concordis
concursus, concursūs, m. — running
    together, gathering
condere — hide, establish, found:
    condit, condidit, conditus
cōnferre — bring together: cōnfert,
    contulit, conlātus
cōnferre gradum — match one's
    step, walk beside
coniūnx, coniugis, m.f. — husband,
    wife
cōnsanguineus, cōnsanguinea,
    cōnsanguineum — of the same
    blood, brother
cōnsilium, cōnsiliī, n. — council,
    meeting
cōnsistere — stop: cōnsistit, cōnstitit
cōnspicere — catch sight of: cōnspicit,
    cōnspexit, cōnspectus
cōnsul, cōnsulis, m. — consul (holder
    of the chief political office)
contendere — strive, compete:
    contendit, contendit
continuō — at once
contrā + Form B (accusative) — in
    answer to
contus, contī, m. — pole
convallis, convallis, f. — valley
cor, cordis, n. — heart
cōram — face to face
corneus, cornea, corneum — made of
    horn

corpus, corporis, n. — body
corripere — seize: corripit, corripuit,
    correptus
sē corripere — take oneself off,
    hasten away
Cossus, Cossī, m. — a famous Roman
    general
crēdere — believe: crēdit, crēdidit,
    crēditus
crimen, crīminis, n. — charge,
    accusation
crīnis, crīnis, m. — hair
crūdēlis, crūdēlis, crūdēle — cruel
crūdus, crūda, crūdum — fresh,
    vigorous
cruentus, cruenta, cruentum — bloody
cubīle, cubīlis, n. — bed, lair
cum + Form E (ablative) — with
cumba, cumbae, f. — boat
cūnctārī — delay: cūnctātur, cūnctātus
    est
cupere — desire, long for: cupit,
    cupīvit, cupītus
cupīdō, cupīdinis, f. — desire
cūra, cūrae, f. — care, anxiety, concern
currus, currūs, m. — chariot
cursus, cursūs, m. — journey, voyage
custōs, custōdis, m. — guard
Cyclōpes, Cyclōpum, m.pl. — Cyclopes,
    a race of one-eyed giants

D

damnāre — condemn: damnat,
    damnāvit, damnātus
Danaī, Danaōrum, m.pl. — Greeks
Dardanidae, Dardanidārum, m.pl. —
    Trojans, descendants of
    Dardanus
Dardanus, Dardanī, m. — Dardanus,
    founder of Troy
dare — give, grant: dat, dedit, datus
dē + Form E (ablative) — from, down
    from
dēbellāre — crush in war, subdue:
    dēbellat, dēbellāvit,
    dēbellātus

41

dēbēre — owe, be due: dēbet, dēbuit,
  dēbitus
dēdūcere — lead away, remove:
  dēdūcit, dēdūxit, dēductus
dēfīgere — fix downwards: dēfīgit,
  dēfīxit, dēfīxus
dēfungī + Form E (ablative) — finish
  with, end: dēfungitur,
  dēfūnctus est
deinde — then, next
dēmēns — mad: dēmentis
dēmittere — let fall, shed: dēmittit,
  dēmīsit, dēmissus
dēmum — at last
dēpendēre — hang down: dēpendet,
  dēpendit
dēpōnere — put down: dēpōnit,
  dēpōsuit, dēpositus
dēscendere — go down, descend:
  dēscendit, dēscendit,
  (dēscēnsūrus)
dēscrībere — describe, trace: dēscrībit,
  dēscrīpsit, dēscrīptus
dēturbāre — turn out: dēturbat,
  dēturbāvit, dēturbātus
deus, deī, m. — god
dēvenīre — come down to: dēvēnit,
  dēvēnit, (dēventūrus)
dexter, dextra, dextrum — right
  dextra, dextrae, f. — right hand
dī — see deus
dicere — say, speak, tell: dīcit, dīxit,
  dictus
dictum, dictī, n. — word
Dīdō, Dīdōnis, f. — Dido, former queen
  of Carthage
diēs, diēī, m.f. — day
digitus, digitī, m. — finger
dignus, digna, dignum + Form E
  (ablative) — worthy of
dīnumerāre — count, calculate:
  dīnumerat, dīnumerāvit,
  dīnumerātus
Dis, Dītis, m. — the god Dis or Pluto,
  lord of the Underworld
discere — learn: discit, didicit

discessus; discessūs, m. — departure
discordia, discordiae, f. — discord,
  strife
discrīmen, discrīminis, n. — distinction,
  separation, difference
dīva, dīvae, f. — goddess
dīverberāre — slash, carve up:
  dīverberat, dīverberāvit,
  dīverberātus
dīvus, dīvī, m. — god
docēre — teach, tell: docet, docuit,
  doctus
doctus, docta, doctum — learned, wise
dolor, dolōris, m. — grief, pain
domina, dominae, f. — mistress
domus, domūs, f. — house, home
dōnum, dōnī, n. — gift
dubitāre — hesitate: dubitat, dubitāvit
dūcere — lead, draw, think: dūcit,
  dūxit, ductus
dulcis, dulcis, dulce — sweet, dear
dum — while
duo, duae, duo — two
dūrus, dūra, dūrum — hard, grim

E

eburnus, eburna, eburnum — made of
  ivory
ecce — see!
ēdūcere — draw out, forge: ēdūcit,
  ēdūxit, ēductus
effugere — escape: effugit, effūgit
effundere — pour out: effundit,
  effūdit, effūsus
egestās, egestātis, f. — need, poverty
ego, meī — I
ēheu — alas
elephantus, elephantī, m. — elephant,
  ivory
ēmittere — send out: ēmittit, ēmīsit,
  ēmissus
enim — for
ēnumerāre — count over: ēnumerat,
  ēnumerāvit, ēnumerātus
Eōus, Eōa, Eōum — of the East,
  eastern

equidem — indeed
equus, equī, m. — horse
Erebus, Erebī, m. — the Underworld
ergō — therefore
Ēridanus, Ēridanī, m. — the river
   Eridanus
Eriphȳlē, Eriphȳlēs, f. — Eriphyle, a
   victim of an unhappy love
   affair
errāre — wander: errat, errāvit
ēructāre — throw up: ēructat, ēructāvit
Erymanthus, Erymanthī, m. —
   Erymanthus, a mountain range
   in Greece
esse — be: est, fuit, (futūrus)
et — and, too
   et ... et — both ... and
etiam — even, also
Eumenides, Eumenidum, f.pl. — the
   Furies
ēvādere — go out, pass beyond: ēvādit,
   ēvāsit, (ēvāsūrus)
Ēvadnē, Ēvadnēs, f. — Evadne, a victim
   of an unhappy love affair
ex + Form E (ablative) — out of, from
excidere — fall from, tumble out:
   excidit, excidit
excolere — improve, enhance: excolit,
   excoluit, excultus
excūdere — beat out, forge: excūdit,
   excūdit, excūsus
exercēre — exercise: exercet, exercuit,
   exercitus
exigere — force, complete: exigit,
   exēgit, exāctus
exiguus, exigua, exiguum — small, thin,
   ghostly
exim = exinde — then, after that
exitus, exitūs, m. — way out
exoptāre — long for: exoptat,
   exoptāvit, exoptātus
expōnere — put out, put ashore:
   expōnit, exposuit, expositus
exsanguis, exsanguis, exsangue —
   bloodless, pale
exsors + Form D (genitive) — without a

part of, having no share in:
   exsortis
exspectāre — wait for, expect:
   exspectat, exspectāvit,
   exspectātus
exstinguere — extinguish, kill:
   exstinguit, exstīnxit,
   exstīnctus
extendere — stretch out: extendit,
   extendit, extentus
extrā + Form B (accusative) — beyond,
   outside
extrēmus, extrēma, extrēmum — last

F

Fabiī, Fabiōrum, m.pl. — the Fabii, a
   distinguished Roman family
Fābricius, Fābriciī, m. — Fabricius, a
   famous Roman general
facere — do, make: facit, fēcit, factus
facilis, facilis, facile — easy
factum, factī, n. — deed
fallere — deceive, be false: fallit,
   fefellit, falsus
falsus, falsa, falsum — false
fāma, fāmae, f. — fame, glory
famēs, famis, f. — hunger
fārī — speak: fātur, fātus est
fās, n. — right, divine law
fascēs, fascium, m.pl. — bundles of
   rods, symbolising political
   power
fātālis, fātālis, fātāle — of destiny,
   fateful
fātum, fātī, n. — fate, destiny, death
faucēs, faucium, f.pl. — jaws, entrance
fēmina, fēminae, f. — woman
fera, ferae, f. — wild beast
ferre — bring, bear, say, lead: fert,
   tulit, lātus
   sē ferre — make one's way
ferreus, ferrea, ferreum — made of iron
ferrūgineus, ferrūginea, ferrūgineum —
   rust-coloured, dark
ferrum, ferrī, n. — iron, sword
fessus, fessa, fessum — weary

fidēs, fidēi, f. — good faith, trust,
  honour
figere — fix, pierce: figit, fixit, fixus
figūra, figūrae, f. — shape
flamma, flammae, f. — flame
flectere — bend, turn: flectit, flexit,
  flexus
flēre — weep: flet, flēvit, flētus
flētus, flētūs, m. — weeping, tears
flōs, flōris, m. — flower
fluentum, fluentī, n. — stream
flūmen, flūminis, n. — river
fluvius, fluviī, m. — river
folium, foliī, n. — leaf
forēs, forium, f.pl. — door
fōrma, fōrmae, f. — shape, appearance
formīdō, formīdinis, f. — fear, terror
fornix, fornicis, m. — arch
forte — by chance
fortūna, fortūnae, f. — fortune,
  destiny
fortūnātus, fortūnāta, fortūnātum —
  lucky, happy, blessed
forus, forī, m. — gangway
frequēns — frequent, in a crowd:
  frequentis
frequentāre — crowd, resort to, throng:
  frequentat, frequentāvit,
  frequentātus
frīgidus, frīgida, frīgidum — icy, cold
frīgus, frīgoris, n. — cold
frūgēs, frūgum, f.pl. — corn, grain
frūstrā — in vain
frūstrārī — frustrate, mock, fool:
  frūstrātur, frūstrātus est
fugāre — put to flight, drive: fugat,
  fugāvit, fugātus
fugere — run away: fugit, fūgit
fulgēre — shine, gleam: fulget, fulsit
fulmen, fulminis, n. — thunderbolt
fulvus, fulva, fulvum — yellow,
  tawny
fundere — pour out, spread out:
  fundit, fūdit, fūsus
fūnus, fūneris, n. — death
futūrus — see esse

G

Garamantes, Garamantum, m.pl. —
  Garamantes, a people of North
  Africa
gaudium, gaudiī, n. — joy
gemere — groan: gemit, gemuit
geminus, gemina, geminum — twin,
  two
gena, genae, f. — cheek
gener, generis, m. — son-in-law
generāre — beget: generat, generāvit,
  generātus
genitor, genitōris, m. — father
gēns, gentis, f. — family, people
genus, generis, n. — race, descent
gerere — do, fight: gerit, gessit, gestus
gignere — bear, give birth to: gignit,
  genuit, genitus
glaucus, glauca, glaucum — grey
Glaucus, Glaucī, m. — Glaucus, a
  Trojan hero
glomerāre — gather together, flock:
  glomerat, glomerāvit,
  glomerātus
Gorgones, Gorgonum, f.pl. — the
  Gorgons, three hideous sisters
  whose gaze turned men to stone
Gracchus, Gracchī, m. — Gracchus, the
  father of the Gracchus brothers
gradī — step, walk: graditur, gressus est
gradus, gradūs, m. — step
grāmen, grāminis, n. — grass
grāmineus, grāminea, grāmineum —
  grassy
grātia, grātiae, f. — pleasure
gressus, gressūs, m. — step
gurges, gurgitis, m. — whirlpool, flood
guttur, gutturis, n. — throat

H

habēna, habēnae, f. — rein
habitāre — live, dwell: habitat,
  habitāvit
haerēre — stick, cling: haeret, haesit,
  haesus
harēna, harēnae, f. — sand

Harpȳiae, Harpȳiārum, f.pl. – the Harpies, half women and half vultures
hasta, hastae, f. – spear
herba, herbae, f. – grass
hērōs, hērōis, m. – hero
heu = ēheu – alas
hiāre – gape: hiat, hiāvit
hīc – here, then
hic, haec, hoc – this: huius
hinc – from here
horrendus, horrenda, horrendum – dreadful
horrēre – bristle, tremble: horret, horruit
horrēscere – tremble at, shudder: horrēscit, horruit
hūc – here, to this place
humus, humī, f. – ground

I
iacere – throw: iacit, iēcit, iactus
iacēre – lie: iacet, iacuit
iactāre – toss, buffet: iactat, iactāvit, iactātus
iam – now, already
iam . . . iam – at one time . . . at another time
iampridem – for a long time now
iānitor, iānitōris, m. – doorkeeper
ibi – then, there
Īdaeus, Īdaeī, m. – Idaeus, a Trojan hero
īdem, eadem, idem – the same: eiusdem
ille, illa, illud – he, she, it, that: illīus
Īlus, Īlī, m. – Ilus, grandfather of Priam
imāgō, imāginis, f. – ghost, likeness, form, image
immānis, immānis, immāne – huge, monstrous
immēnsus, immēnsa, immēnsum – immeasurable, great
immittere – send into: immittit, immisit, immissus

imperium, imperiī, n. – command, empire, dominion
impōnere – put on, set on: impōnit, imposuit, impositus
īmus, īma, īmum – lowest, deepest
in + Form B (accusative) – in, into, towards, against, onto
in + Form E (ablative) – in, on
inamābilis, inamābilis, inamābile – hateful, unlovely
inānis, inānis, ināne – empty
incendere – set light to, inflame: incendit, incendit, incēnsus
incertus, incerta, incertum – uncertain, fitful
incipere – begin: incipit, incēpit, inceptus
inclūdere – shut in, enclose, confine: inclūdit, inclūsit, inclūsus
inclutus, incluta, inclutum – famed, glorious
incolumis, incolumis, incolume – safe
increpāre – rebuke: increpat, increpuit, increpitus
incultus, inculta, incultum – untrimmed, unkempt
inde – from there, then
Indī, Indōrum, m.pl. – Indians
īnfāns, īnfantis, m.f. – baby
īnfēlīx – unlucky, wretched: īnfēlīcis
īnfōrmis, īnfōrmis, īnfōrme – shapeless
ingemere – groan: ingemit, ingemuit
ingēns – huge: ingentis
inhumātus, inhumāta, inhumātum – unburied
inimīcus, inimīca, inimīcum – hostile, unfriendly
inīquus, inīqua, inīquum – unfair, cruel
innexus, innexa, innexum – bound
innumerus, innumera, innumerum – countless
innūptus, innūpta, innūptum – unwed
inops – poor, helpless: inopis
inremeābilis, inremeābilis, inremeābile – not to be crossed again

45

inruere − rush at: inruit, inruit

inscius, inscia, inscium − ignorant, not
    knowing

insidere,+ Form C (dative) − settle on:
    insidit, insedit, (insessurus)

insidiae, insidiarum, f.pl. − ambush,
    surprise attack

insignis, insignis, insigne − famous,
    outstanding

insomnium, insomnii, n. − dream

insons − guiltless: insontis

instruere − draw up: instruit, instruxit,
    instructus

inter + Form B (accusative) − between,
    among

interea − meanwhile

interfusus, interfusa, interfusum −
    flowing between

invenire − find, discover: invenit,
    invenit, inventus

invictus, invicta, invictum −
    unconquered

invitus, invita, invitum − unwilling,
    reluctant

ipse, ipsa, ipsum − himself, herself,
    itself: ipsius

ira, irae, f. − anger

ire − go: it, iit, (iturus)

istinc − from there

Italia, Italiae, f. − Italy

iter, itineris, n. − journey

iubere − order: iubet, iussit, iussus

iudex, iudicis, m. − judge

iugum, iugi, n. − ridge, yoke, rowing-
    bench

iungere − join: iungit, iunxit,
    iunctus

Iuppiter, Iovis, m. − Jupiter

iurare − swear: iurat, iuravit, iuratus

iussum, iussi, n. − order

iuvare − help, please: iuvat, iuvit,
    (iuvaturus)

iuvenis, iuvenis, m. − young man

iuxta − next, nearby

iuxta + Form B (accusative) − next
    to

L

labi − fall: labitur, lapsus est

labos, laboris, m. − work, toil

lacrima, lacrimae, f. − tear

lacus, lacus, m. − lake

laetari − be glad, rejoice: laetatur,
    laetatus est

laetus, laeta, laetum − happy, glad

laevus, laeva, laevum − left
    laeva, laevae, f. − left hand

Laodamia, Laodamiae, f. − Laodamia,
    a victim of an unhappy love
    affair

largus, larga, largum − generous,
    spacious

latere − lie hidden: latet, latuit

latex, laticis, m. − liquid, water

Latinus, Latini, m. − Latinus, king of
    Latium

Latium, Latii, n. − Latium

latrare − bark: latrat, latravit

latratus, latratus, m. − barking

latus, lata, latum − wide, broad

Laurentes, Laurentum, m.pl. −
    Laurentians, an Italian tribe

laurus, lauri (-us), f. − laurel, bay

laus, laudis, f. − praise

laxare − make loose, relax: laxat,
    laxavit, laxatus

lenire − soothe, soften: lenit, lenivit

Lerna, Lernae, f. − Lerna, near Argos,
    where Hercules killed the Hydra

Lethaeus, Lethaea, Lethaeum − of the
    Lethe, one of the rivers of the
    Underworld

letum, leti, n. − death

levis, levis, leve − light

Liber, Liberi, m. − the god Liber, also
    known as Bacchus or Dionysus

libertas, libertatis, f. − freedom

Libya, Libyae, f. − Libya, North
    Africa.

licere − be permitted, may: licet, licuit

licet − although

lilium, lilii, n. − lily

limen, liminis, n. − doorstep, threshold

46

līmes, līmitis, m. – path, course
līmus, līmī, m. – mud
linquere – leave: linquit, līquit
lītus, lītoris, n. – shore
līvidus, līvida, līvidum – lead-coloured, dark
locus, locī, m. – place
longaevus, longaeva, longaevum – aged
longē – far away, at a distance
longus, longa, longum – long, long-lasting
loquī – speak: loquitur, locūtus est
luctārī – struggle: luctātur, luctātus est
lūctus, lūctūs, m. – grief
lūdus, lūdī, m. – game, sport
lūgēre – mourn, grieve: lūget, lūxit
lūmen, lūminis, n. – light
    pl. eyes
lūna, lūnae, f. – moon
lūstrāre – survey, scan: lūstrat, lūstrāvit, lūstrātus
lūx, lūcis, f. – light, daylight

M
Maeōtius, Maeōtia, Maeōtium – Maeotian, Scythian
maestus, maesta, maestum – sad, unhappy
magis – more
magnanimus, magnanima, magnanimum – great-spirited
magnus, magna, magnum – big, great
malesuādus, malesuāda, malesuādum – evil-counselling
malignus, maligna, malignum – grudging
malus, mala, malum – bad, evil, wicked
manēre – remain: manet, mānsit, (mānsūrus)
Mānēs, Mānium, m.pl. – spirits of the dead
manus, manūs, f. – hand, band of men
marmor, marmoris, n. – marble
Marpēsius, Marpēsia, Marpēsium – from Marpessus, a mountain

famous for marble on the island of Paros
māter, mātris, f. – mother
Maximus, Maximī, m. – Quintus Fabius Maximus Cunctator, the most famous of the Fabii
meātus, meātūs, m. – movement
medicātus, medicāta, medicātum – drugged
medius, media, medium – middle, mid
Medōn, Medontis, m. – Medon, a Trojan hero
mel, mellis, n. – honey
melior, melius – see bonus, bene
membrum, membrī, n. – limb
meminisse – remember: meminit
memor – mindful, keeping in mind: memoris
memorāre – speak of, say: memorat, memorāvit, memorātus
mēns, mentis, f. – mind
mēnsis, mēnsis, m. – month
mentum, mentī, n. – chin
merēre – deserve: meret, meruit, meritus
mergere – plunge, immerse: mergit, mersit, mersus
metuere – fear: metuit, metuit
metus, metūs, m. – fear
meus, mea, meum – my
    meī, meōrum, m.pl. – my people
ministrāre – attend to: ministrat, ministrāvit
minōrēs, minōrum, m.pl. – descendants
Mīnōs, Mīnōis, m. – King Minos, judge of the dead
minus – less
    nec minus – nevertheless
mirārī – wonder at: mirātur, mirātus est
miserārī – pity: miserātur, miserātus est
mittere – send: mittit, mīsit, missus
moenia, moenium, n.pl. – walls
mōlīrī – toil at: mōlītur, mōlītus est

47

molliter — softly, smoothly
  mollius
mônstrâre — point out, show, display:
  mônstrat, mônstrâvit,
  mônstrâtus
mônstrum, mônstrî, n. — strange shape,
  monster
morârî — delay: morâtur, morâtus est
morbus, morbî, m. — disease
mors, mortis, f. — death
mortifer, mortifera, mortiferum —
  death-bringing
môs, môris, m. — custom, way
movêre — move, disturb: movet, môvit,
  môtus
multus, multa, multum — many, much
  plûs — more: plûris
  plûrimus, plûrima, plûrimum —
  very many, most
mûnus, mûneris, n. — gift, duty, task
murmur, murmuris, n. — murmuring,
  buzzing
myrteus, myrtea, myrteum — of
  myrtle

N
nâscî — be born: nâscitur, nâtus est
nâtus, nâtî, m. — son
nauta, nautae, m. — sailor, boatman
nâvis, nâvis, f. — ship, boat
nâvita = nauta
nê — lest, in order that . . . not
nê = nôlî or nôlîte
nec — nor, and not
  nec . . . nec — neither . . . nor
  nec nôn — and also
nefâs, n. — crime, wrong
nemus, nemoris, n. — wood, grove
nepôs, nepôtis, m. — grandson,
  descendant
neu = nêve — and . . . not, nor
nî = nisi
Nîlus, Nîli, m. — the river Nile
nisi — if not, unless, except
nitêns — shining, glossy: nitentis
niveus, nivea, niveum — snow-white

nocêre + Form C (dative) — harm:
  nocet, nocuit
nôdus, nôdî, m. — knot
nômen, nôminis, n. — name
nôn — not
nôs, nostrum — we, us
nôscere — get to know: nôscit, nôvit,
  nôtus
noster, nostra, nostrum — our
nôtus, nôta, nôtum — well-known,
  familiar
noviês — nine times
novus, nova, novum — new, strange,
  fresh
nox, noctis, f. — night
nûbila, nûbilôrum, n.pl. — clouds
nûllus, nûlla, nûllum — no
nûmen, nûminis, n. — divine power
numerus, numerî, m. — number,
  rhythm
nunc — now
nûntius, nûntiî, m. — message
Nŷsa, Nŷsae, f. — Mount Nysa

O
ô — O!
ob — on account of, for
obicere — throw to: obicit, obiêcit,
  obiectus
obîre — travel over: obit, obiit, obitus
oblivia, oblîviôrum, n.pl. —
  forgetfulness
obloquî — play as an accompaniment:
  obloquitur, oblocûtus est
obscûrus, obscûra, obscûrum — dim,
  dark
obstâre — stand in the way: obstat,
  obstitit
occupâre — seize possession of:
  occupat, occupâvit, occupâtus
occurrere + Form C (dative) — run to
  meet: occurrit, occurrit
oculus, oculî, m. — eye
odôrâtus, odôrâta, odôrâtum —
  scented, fragrant
offa, offae, f. — titbit, morsel

offerre — offer: offert, obtulit, oblātus
ollī = illī
Olympus, Olympī, m. — Mount
    Olympus, home of the gods
omnis, omnis, omne — all, every
opācus, opāca, opācum — shady,
    shadowed, dark
ōrāre — beg, plead: ōrat, ōrāvit, ōrātus
Orcus, Orcī, m. — the Underworld
ōrdō, ōrdinis, m. — rank, line
ōs, ōris, n. — mouth, face
os, ossis, n. — bone
ostendere — show: ostendit, ostendit,
    ostentus
ōstium, ōstiī, n. — door, mouth of river

P

pācāre — tame, pacify: pācat, pācāvit,
    pācātus
paeān, paeānis, m. — hymn of praise
palaestra, palaestrae, f. — wrestling-
    ground, palaestra
pallēns — pale: pallentis
palma, palmae, f. — palm, hand
palūs, palūdis, f. — marsh
pampineus, pampinea, pampineum —
    of vine tendrils
pandere — spread, open: pandit,
    pandit, passus
pār — like, equal: paris
parcere + Form C (dative) — spare:
    parcit, pepercit, parsus
parēns, parentis, m.f. — parent
parere — produce, bring about: parit,
    peperit, partus
pariter — alike, side by side
pars, partis, f. — part
Parthenopaeus, Parthenopaeī, m. —
    Parthenopaeus, a hero who
    fought in the war known as
    Seven against Thebes
parvus, parva, parvum — small, little
pāscere — feed, graze: pāscit, pāvit,
    pāstus
Pāsiphaē, Pāsiphaēs, f. — Pasiphae, a
    victim of an unhappy love affair

passim — everywhere, here and there
pater, patris, m. — father
patī — suffer, endure: patitur, passus
    est
patria, patriae, f. — fatherland, native
    country
patruus, patruī, m. — uncle
pauperiēs, pauperiēī, f. — poverty
pāx, pācis, f. — peace
pecten, pectinis, m. — plectrum
penitus + Form E (ablative) — deep in
peperit — see parere
per + Form B (accusative) — through,
    along
peragere — carry through, continue:
    peragit, perēgit, perāctus
percutere — strike, shatter: percutit,
    percussit, percussus
perēsse — eat away: peredit, perēdit,
    perēsus
perferre — endure: perfert, pertulit,
    perlātus
perficere — finish, complete: perficit,
    perfēcit, perfectus
periclum = periculum
periculum, periculī, n. — danger
perōsus, perōsa, perōsum — hating
personāre — make resound: personat,
    personuit
pēs, pedis, m. — foot
petere — seek, make for: petit, petīvit,
    petītus
Phaedra, Phaedrae, f. — Phaedra, a
    victim of an unhappy love affair
phalanx, phalangis, f. — phalanx,
    battle line
Phoebus, Phoebī, m. — Apollo, god of
    prophecy
Phoenissus, Phoenissa, Phoenissum —
    Phoenician
pietās, pietātis, f. — sense of duty,
    devotion, goodness
Pīrithous, Pīrithoī, m. — Pirithous, a
    friend of Theseus
pius, pia, pium — dutiful, good, holy
placidus, placida, placidum — peaceful

plaudere — beat out, tread: plaudit,
    plausit, plausus
plūs, plūris: plūrimus — see multus
poena, poenae, f. — punishment
Polyboetēs, Polyboetae, m. —
    Polyboetes, a Trojan hero
pondus, ponderis, n. — weight
pōnere — place, lay down: pōnit,
    posuit, positus
pontus, ponti, m. — sea
populus, populī, m. — people
porrō — far off, at a distance
porta, portae, f. — gate
portitor, portitōris, m. — ferryman
portus, portūs, m. — harbour
post — afterwards
postquam — after
pōtāre — drink: pōtat, pōtāvit,
    pōtātus
potēns — powerful: potentis
praeceptum, praeceptī, n. — order,
    command
praenatāre — flow past: praenatat,
    praenatāvit
praetereā — besides
prātum, prātī, n. — meadow
premere — check, press, weigh down:
    premit, pressit, pressus
prīmum — first
    ut prīmum — as soon as
prīmus, prīma, prīmum — first
prior, prior, prius — earlier, first
pristinus, pristina, pristinum — former
prius quam — before
prō + Form E (ablative) — for the sake
    of
procer, proceris, m. — chief
Procris, Procris, f. — Procris, a victim
    of an unhappy love affair
procul — in the distance, far
prōferre — extend: prōfert, prōtulit,
    prōlātus
profundus, profunda, profundum —
    deep
prohibēre — prevent: prohibet,
    prohibuit, prohibitus

prōicere — throw away: prōicit,
    prōiēcit, prōiectus
prōlēs, prōlis, f. — offspring
prōmittere — promise: prōmittit,
    prōmīsit, prōmissus
propinquāre — approach: propinquat,
    propinquāvit
prōra, prōrae, f. — prow
prōsequī — follow: prōsequitur,
    prōsecūtus est
Prōserpina, Prōserpinae, f. —
    Proserpina, wife of Dis
prōspicere — look out, see far off:
    prōspicit, prōspexit, prōspectus
proximus, proxima, proximum —
    next, nearest
puella, puellae, f. — girl
puer, puerī, m. — boy
pugnāre — fight: pugnat, pugnāvit,
    pugnātus
pulcher, pulchra, pulchrum —
    beautiful, lovely, handsome:
    pulcherrimus
pulsāre — strike: pulsat, pulsāvit,
    pulsātus
puppis, puppis, f. — stern, boat
purpureus, purpurea, purpureum —
    purple, bright
putāre — think: putat, putāvit,
    putātus

Q
quaesītor, quaesītōris, m. — inquisitor
quālis, quālis, quāle — just like, like,
    such as
quam — as, how, than
quamquam — although
quantus, quanta, quantum — how
    great, how much
-que — and
    -que . . . -que — both . . . and
quī, quae, quod — who, which: cuius
quid? — why, how?
quiēscere — become still, rest: quiēscit,
    quiēvit, quiētus
quīre — be able; quit, quīvit

quis, qua, quid — any, anyone,
anything: cuius
quis, quid? — who, what?: cuius
quisque, quidque — each: cuiusque
quisquis, quicquid — whoever,
whatever
quō — where, to what place
quō + subjunctive — so that, to
quō modō — how, in what way
quondam — once

R
rabidus, rabida, rabidum — frenzied
radius, radii, m. — measuring-rod
rāmus, rāmī, m. — branch, bough
rapere — snatch: rapit, rapuit, raptus
ratis, ratis, f. — boat
raucus, rauca, raucum — noisy,
rumbling
recēns — fresh: recentis
recēnsēre — review: recēnset, recēnsuit,
recēnsus
recipere — take back, recover: recipit,
recēpit, receptus
recolere — contemplate: recolit,
recoluit, recultus
rēctus, rēcta, rēctum — straight,
direct
recubāre — lie: recubat, recubuit
reddere — give back, answer: reddit,
reddidit, redditus
reductus, reducta, reductum —
withdrawn, remote
refugere — run back: refugit, refūgit
regere — command, rule: regit, rēxit,
rēctus
rēgīna, rēgīnae, f. — queen
regiō, regiōnis, f. — region, area
rēgnāre — rule, reign: rēgnat, rēgnāvit,
rēgnātus
rēgnum, rēgnī, n. — kingdom
relinquere — leave: relinquit, relīquit,
relictus
rēmus, rēmī, m. — oar
reperīre — discover: reperit, repperit,
repertus

repōnere — lay to rest: repōnit,
reposuit, repositus
requīrere — seek, ask: requīrit,
requīsīvit, requīsītus
rērī — think: rētur, ratus est
rēs, reī, f. — thing, situation
residere — subside: residit, resēdit
resolvere — loosen, unfasten, relax:
resolvit, resolvit, resolūtus
respondēre — reply, answer: respondet,
respondit, (respōnsūrus)
respōnsum, respōnsī, n. — answer,
oracle
restituere — restore: restituit, restituit,
restitūtus
revīsere — return to: revīsit, revīsit,
revīsus
revolvere — turn back: revolvit,
revolvit, revolūtus
rēx, rēgis, m. — king
rigāre — wet: rigat, rigāvit, rigātus
rīmōsus, rīmōsa, rīmōsum — leaky
rīpa, rīpae, f. — bank
rogus, rogī, m. — funeral pyre
Rōmānus, Rōmānī, m. — Roman
ruere — rush: ruit, ruit
rursus — again

S
sacer, sacra, sacrum — sacred
sacerdōs, sacerdōtis, m.f. — priest,
priestess
saeculum, saeculī, n. — generation, age
saepe — often: saepius
saevus, saeva, saevum — savage, cruel
sāl, salis, m. — salt, sea
sanguis, sanguinis, m. — blood
satis — sufficient, enough
Sāturnus, Sāturnī, m. — the god
Saturn who ruled Latium in the
Golden Age
satus, sata, satum — born of, sprung
from
Scipiadae, Scīpiadārum, m.pl. — the
Scipios, famous Roman
statesmen

51

Scylla, Scyllae, f. — Scylla, half woman and half sea-monster
sē — himself, herself, themselves
secāre — cut: secat, secuit, sectus
   viam secāre — make one's way
sēclūsus, sēclūsa, sēclūsum — secluded
sēcrētus, sēcrēta, sēcrētum — set apart, secret
secūris, secūris, f. — axe (symbol of authority)
sēcūrus, sēcūra, sēcūrum — untroubled, care-dispelling
sed — but
sedēre — sit, settle: sedet, sēdit, (sessūrus)
sēdēs, sēdis, f. — seat, resting-place, home
semel — once
senectūs, senectūtis, f. — old age
senior, seniōris, m. — old man
sentus, senta, sentum — rough
septem — seven
septemgeminus, septemgemina, septemgeminum — sevenfold
sepultus, sepulta, sepultum — buried
sequī — follow, pursue: sequitur, secūtus est
serēnus, serēna, serēnum — clear, bright
serere — sow: serit, sēvit, satus
sermō, sermōnis, m. — talk, words
Serrānus, Serrānī, m. — Serranus, a famous Roman statesman
servāre — look after, guard: servat, servāvit, servātus
sēsē = sē
sī — if
Sibylla, Sibyllae, f. — the Sibyl
sīc — thus
sīdus, sīderis, n. — star, constellation
silēns — silent: silentis
silex, silicis, m.f. — flint
silva, silvae, f. — wood
similis, similis, simile — like
   simillimus
simul — at the same time, together with, as soon as

sine + Form E (ablative) — without
singulī, singulae, singula — single, each and every
sistere — stop, set, check: sistit, stitit
situs, sitūs, m. — position, neglect
socer, socerī, m. — father-in-law
socius, sociī, m. — companion
sōl, sōlis, m. — sun
solium, soliī, n. — throne
solum, solī, n. — ground
sōlus, sōla, sōlum — only, alone, lonely
solvere — release, unharness: solvit, solvit, solūtus
somnium, somniī, n. — dream
somnus, somnī, m. — sleep
sonāre — sound, resound, rustle: sonat, sonuit, sonitus
sopor, sopōris, m. — sleep
sopōrātus, sopōrāta, sopōrātum — drowsy, soporific
sopōrus, sopōra, sopōrum — drowsy
sordidus, sordida, sordidum — dirty
sors, sortis, f. — lot, fate
spargere — sprinkle: spargit, sparsit, sparsus
spatium, spatiī, n. — space
spīrāns — breathing, lifelike: spirantis
squālor, squālōris, m. — filth, dirt
stabulāre — be stabled: stabulat, stabulāvit
stāgnum, stāgnī, n. — pool, marsh
stāre — stand, be fixed: stat, stetit
stēlla, stēllae, f. — star
strāgēs, strāgis, f. — destruction, slaughter
strepere — hum: strepit, strepuit
stridere — hiss: strīdit, strīdit
stringere — draw, unsheathe: stringit, strinxit, strictus
studium, studiī, n. — eagerness
Stygius, Stygia, Stygium — of the Styx (a river in the Underworld)
Styx, Stygis, f. — the river Styx in the Underworld
sub + Form E (ablative) — under, beneath

subicere — conquer: subicit, subiēcit,
    subiectus
subigere — compel, push along, subigit,
    subēgit, subāctus
subitus, subita, subitum — sudden,
    unexpected
subtrahere — withdraw: subtrahit,
    subtrāxit, subtractus
subvectāre — carry, transport:
    subvectat, subvectāvit
sulcus, sulcī, m. — furrow
summovēre — move away, send away:
    summovet, summōvit,
    summōtus
super + Form B (accusative) — over
superbus, superba, superbum —
    proud
supernē — from above
superus, supera, superum — above, in
    the upper world
    superī, superōrum, m.pl. — the gods
    above
surgere — rise: surgit, surrēxit,
    (surrēctūrus)
suscipere — undertake: suscipit,
    suscēpit, susceptus
sūtilis, sūtilis, sūtile — stitched
suus, sua, suum — his, her, its, their
    suī, suōrum, m.pl. — his people
Sychaeus, Sychaeī, m. — Sychaeus,
    once king of Phoenicia

T
tābēs, tābis, f. — wasting away
tacitus, tacita, tacitum — silent
tālis, tālis, tāle — such
tandem — at last
tantus, tanta, tantum — so much, so
    great
Tarquinius, Tarquiniī, m. — Tarquin,
    name of two kings of Rome
Tartareus, Tartarea, Tartareum — of
    Tartarus, the Underworld
tegere — cover: tegit, tēxit, tēctus
tellūs, tellūris, f. — earth, land
tēlum, tēlī, n. — weapon

tempora, temporum, n.pl. — brow,
    temples (of the head)
tempus, temporis, n. — time
tendere — stretch out: tendit, tetendit,
    tentus
tendere ad + Form B (accusative) —
    make for, approach
tenēre — hold, occupy: tenet, tenuit,
    tentus
tenuis, tenuis, tenue — thin,
    insubstantial
ter — three times
tergum, tergī, n. — back
terra, terrae, f. — earth, land
terrēre — frighten: terret, terruit,
    territus
terribilis, terribilis, terribile — dreadful
Teucer, Teucrī, m. — Teucer, ancestor
    of the Trojans
thalamus, thalamī, m. — room, bridal
    chamber
Thersilochus, Thersilochī, m. —
    Thersilochus, a Trojan hero
Thēseus, Thēseī, m. — Theseus, a
    heroic king of Athens
Thrēicius, Thrēicia, Thrēicium —
    Thracian
tigris, tigris, m.f. — tiger
timēre — be afraid of, fear: timet,
    timuit
tollere — raise, destroy: tollit, sustulit,
    sublātus
torquēre — twist, turn: torquet, torsit,
    tortus
torvus, torva, torvum — fierce
tōtus, tōta, tōtum — whole: tōtīus
trahere — drag: trahit, trāxit, tractus
trāns + Form B (accusative) — across
trānsmittere — send across: trānsmittit,
    trānsmīsit, trānsmissus
trānsportāre — carry across:
    trānsportat, trānsportāvit,
    trānsportātus
tremefacere —make tremble:
    tremefacit, tremefēcit,
    tremefactus

tremere — tremble: tremit, tremuit
trepidāre — panic: trepidat, trepidāvit
trepidus, trepida, trepidum — alarmed
trēs, trēs, tria — three
tricorpor — three-bodied: tricorporis
trifaux — three-throated: trifaucis
tristis, tristis, triste — sad, gloomy
Troia, Troiae, f. — Troy
Troius, Troia, Troium — Trojan
tū, tui — you
tuērī — look, look at: tuētur, tuitus est
tum — then
tumidus, tumida, tumidum — swelling
tumultus, tumultūs, m. — uproar,
    confusion
turba, turbae, f. — crowd
turbāre — throw into confusion, be in
    confusion: turbat, turbāvit,
    turbātus
turbidus, turbida, turbidum —
    confused, thick
turpis, turpis, turpe — disgraceful, foul
tuus, tua, tuum — your
Tȳdeus, Tȳdeī, m. — Tydeus
Tyrrhēnus, Tyrrhēna, Tyrrhēnum —
    Tyrrhenian

U
ūber, ūberis, n. — breast
ubi — where, when
ulmus, ulmī, f. — elm
ulterior — further: ulteriōris
ultimus, ultima, ultimum — last,
    furthest
ultor, ultōris, m. — avenger
ultrīx — avenging: ultrīcis
ultrō — of one's own accord
ulva, ulvae, f. — sedge, rushes
umbra, umbrae, f. — shadow, shade,
    ghost
umbrifer, umbrifera, umbriferum —
    shadowy
umerus, umerī, m. — shoulder
ūnā — together
unda, undae, f. — wave, water
unde — from where

ūnus, ūna, ūnum — one: ūnīus
urbs, urbis, f. — city
urna, urnae, f. — urn, jar
usque — continually, indefinitely, for a
    long time
ut + indicative — as, when
utcumque — however
uterque, utraque, utrumque — each (of
    two), both

V
vacuus, vacua, vacuum — empty
vada, vadōrum, n.pl. — shallows
vagārī — wander: vagātur, vagātus est
vāgītus, vāgītūs, m. — wailing
validus, valida, validum — strong
vallis, vallis, f. — valley
vānus, vāna, vānum — empty,
    meaningless
varius, varia, varium — varied, different
vāstus, vāsta, vāstum — huge
vātēs, vātis, m.f. — prophet,
    prophetess
-ve — or
vectāre — carry, transport: vectat,
    vectāvit
vehere — carry, convey: vehit, vēxit,
    vectus
vehī — travel, ride
vel — or
velle — wish, want, be willing: vult,
    voluit
vēlum, vēlī, n. — sail
velutī = velut — as if, just like
venerābilis, venerābilis, venerābile — to
    be revered, awesome
venīre — come: venit, vēnit, (ventūrus)
ventus, ventī, m. — wind
vērō — indeed
verrere — sweep: verrit, verrit, versus
vertere — turn, turn round: vertit,
    vertit, versus
vertex, verticis, m. — summit, top
vērus, vēra, vērum — true
vescī — feed, feast: vescitur
vestibulum, vestibulī, n. — entrance

54

vestigium, vestigii, n. — trace, footstep, step
vestire — clothe: vestit, vestivit, vestitus
vestis, vestis, f. — garment
vetus — old: veteris
via, viae, f. — way, road
victor — victorious: victoris
videre — see: videt, vidit, visus
vincere — overcome, conquer: vincit, vicit, victus
vinclum = vinculum
vinculum, vinculi, n. — bond, chain
vipereus, viperea, vipereum — snaky
vir, viri, m. — man, husband
virecta, virectorum, n.pl. — green places, lawns
virens — green: virentis
virga, virgae, f. — rod, branch
virgo, virginis, f. — virgin, girl
virgulta, virgultorum, n.pl. — thickets, undergrowth

viridis, viridis, viride — green
virtus, virtutis, f. — courage
vis, f. — force
pl. vires — strength
viscera, viscerum, n.pl. — flesh and blood, heart
visus, visus, m. — sight
vita, vitae, f. — life
vitta, vittae, f. — headband
vivus, viva, vivum — alive, living
vocare — call: vocat, vocavit, vocatus
volare — fly: volat, volavit
volitare — fly, flutter: volitat, volitavit
volucer, volucris, volucre — winged
volvi — roll, flow: volvitur, volutus est
vorago, voraginis, f. — abyss, chasm
vox, vocis, f. — voice, cry
vulgo — commonly
vulnus, vulneris, n. — wound
vultus, vultus, m. — face, expression

55